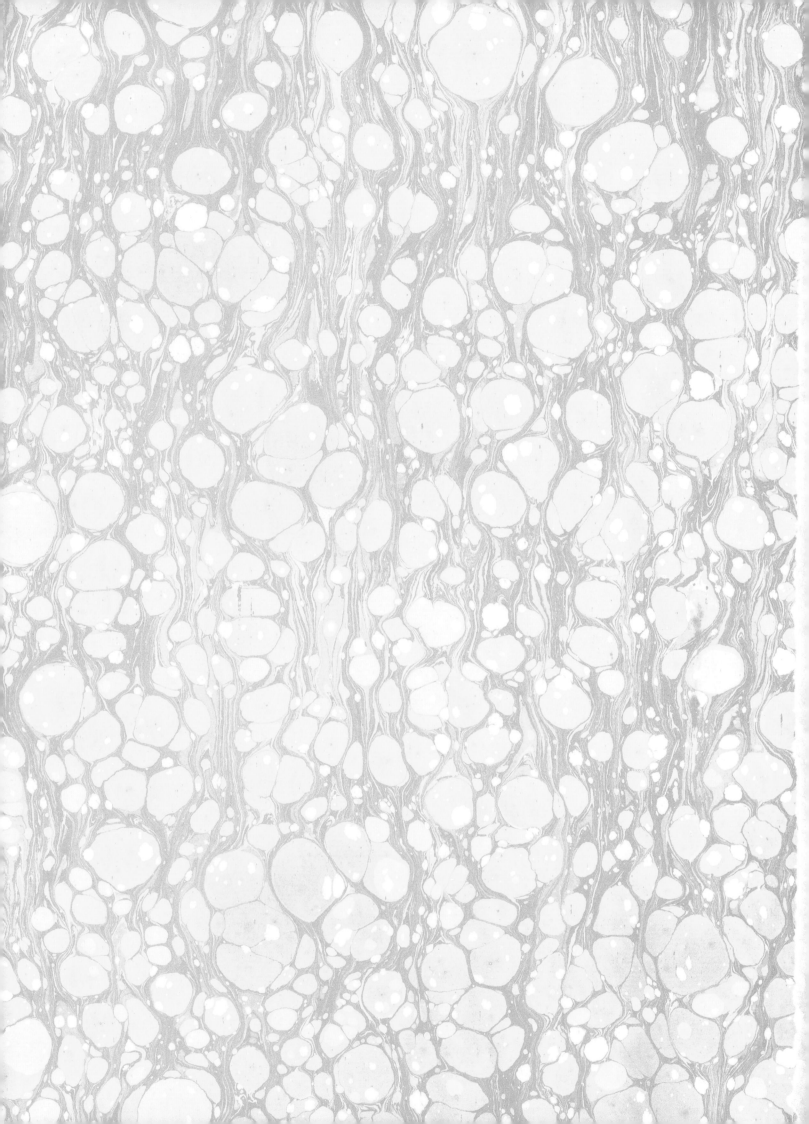

ART DIRECTORS CLUB OF LOS ANGELES
7080 Hollywood Blvd., Suite 410
Los Angeles, California 90028
213/465-8707

Executive Director   *Barbara Shore*

Distributors to the trade
in the United States
and Canada:
Watson-Guptill
Publications
1515 Broadway
New York, N.Y. 10036

Distributed throughout
the rest of the world by:
Hearst Publications
International
105 Madison Avenue
New York, N.Y. 10016

PUBLISHER:
Madison Square Press
10 East 23rd Street
New York, N.Y. 10010

Printed in Japan

ISBN 0-8230-5829-8

ADLA:5 CREDITS

COVER AND
BOOK DESIGN . . . . *Jeri Heiden*

BOOK COMMITTEE . . . . *Jeri Heiden*
  Linda Cobb
  Kim Champagne
  Christine Cano
  John Heiden
  Terry Robertson

PROJECT
COORDINATION . . . . *Linda Cobb*

TYPOGRAPHY . . . . *Andresen Typographics*

EDITORIAL ASSISTANT *Melissa Hoel*

PHOTOGRAPHY . . . . *Stuart Watson*

CONTRIBUTORS . . . . *Andresen Typographics*
  Warner Bros. Records

THE 42ND ANNUAL COMPETITION

ADLA FIVE

ART DIRECTORS CLUB OF LOS ANGELES

TABLE OF CONTENTS

INVOLVEMENT in the Art Directors Club of Los Angeles has been a gratifying

experience. As 1987/1988 President, I set goals for the club—to unify and strengthen the organization, and to encourage participation by people in the advertising and design community.

As a means of achieving these goals, quarterly meetings with the Advisory Board were initiated to encourage their involvement in addressing club concerns and its future. Feedback from the likes of Saul Bass and Steve Hayden is always enlightening and frequently provocative. Interest in the club has increased in the advertising sector also, as evidenced by a record breaking number of entrants in the advertising category of this year's competition.

Our 1988 Call for Entries attracted close to 4500 responses, approximately 400 of which appear in this annual; fifty received Special Judges Awards. The Awards Banquet was memorable, enabling the club's officers to meet most of the winners. It also included Lou Dorfsman's presentation of our Lifetime Achievement Award to Saul Bass and an eloquent recap of Saul's career by his partner, Herb Yager.

The past two years have been very rewarding for me. Through the ADLA I have been able to meet truly outstanding individuals from across the country, with common pursuits and interests. I look forward to continued involvement as Chairman of the Club's Advisory Board.

Congratulations to those of you who emerged winners, and thanks to all who entered. Your work has helped reinforce the standards of excellence upon which the Art Directors Club of Los Angeles prides itself.

Dan Lennon
President

ONCE AGAIN, the Art Directors Club of Los Angeles is fortunate to be supported by

members who graciously offer their time and energy. I'm inspired by the continuing encouragement and interest of our members, whose support makes our programs possible and worthwhile. I want to thank my predecessor Jeff Spear for the unselfish hours of work he contributed to this club and all of his achievements that help make this annual possible.

To the volunteers who donated their hundreds of hours to showcase the tens of thousands of hours of work— Thank You. Thank you for helping to enrich our profession by capturing this awarded body of work, and preventing it from slipping away from memory.

About our enlarged panel of judges now numbering twenty—four in design, four in entertainment, four in editorial and eight in advertising (four in print media, four in broadcast media)—they did a great job. Their contribution and dedication to judging the entries supported a high level of competition, making this ADLA annual the best ever.

Gary A. Valenti
Vice President

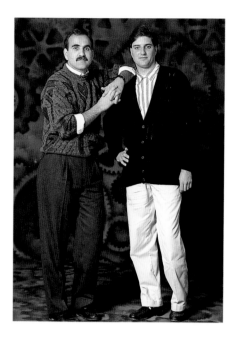

Gary Valenti
Dave Glaze
Banquet Chairmen

On the evening of November 22, 1988 over 400 advertising and design professionals gathered at the Los Angeles Biltmore Hotel to spotlight the 402 winning entries to be included in this year's ADLA:5 Annual.

At the Awards Banquet, Art Goodman and Lou Dorfsman took the podium to announce this year's ADLA Medal for Lifetime Achievement, honoring Saul Bass for his contributions to the industry. Art Goodman shared many humorous stories and slides of Saul's work.

Toni Hollander and Max Goodrich awarded the Annual George Rice and Sons Scholarship, to sixth-term graphic student Ben Guevara attending Art Center College of Design in Pasadena.

The viewing and presentation of awards to the top entries in each category followed. There were 53 awards in the four categories: Advertising, Graphic Design, Editorial and Entertainment; four entries were awarded Best of Show.

Our thanks to those who attended for their continued support, to the hardworking banquet/show committee for their successful efforts, and to The Designory, Inc. for loaning the creative talents of David Glaze and Christine Ferguson. Julie Prendiville from Foote, Cone & Belding also provided valuable help. Also to quick-witted Master of Ceremonies radio funnyman Alan Barzman, who joined us to keep things moving at a hilarious speed.

Another incredible enthusiastic supporter is Craig Butler, who stepped-in to produce a well-received and unique "Off the Wall" exhibition. Craig deserves a special round of applause from our membership for putting on this event.

Craig Butler
Show Chairman

VOLUNTEERS
Stephanie Conner—Show Manager
Carlos Cordova
Nan Faessler
D.D. Hunter
Rick Linstrom
Gayle Miller
Tso

Leah Hoffmitz
Doug Brotherton
Judging Chairpersons

JUDGING COMMITTEE
Anne Burdick
Anne Eichelberger
Laura Gruenther
Mark Harmel
Terry Irwin
Tamara Keith
Steve Kimura
Booker Rinder

The 42nd Annual ADLA Show was judged on August 5-7, 1988. This year's judging was an impressive, grueling and exhilarating event. The process is spaced over a two day period. Entries are catalogued and organized for viewing, by category. Editorial and Entertainment, our two newest categories, took up one day, while the Advertising and Design Categories, because of the quantity of entries and numerous subcategories, took up two days—one for video and slides, the other for print. Scores for the nearly 4,500 entries were tallied and entered into a computer to determine the finalists in each group, and award winners were selected from the finalists by our judges.

The sheer quantity of print and broadcast entries in the Advertising section alone required that ADLA add four judges in both of those categories this year.

Despite the show's size, judges say that their tasks are made easy by the organization and planning which precede the event. The Show's Co-Chairpersons, Leah Hoffmitz and Doug Brotherton, along with the show committee members and the many volunteers, worked to make sure that nothing was overlooked, and that every detail and deadline was met.

VOLUNTEERS

Vicki Adjami
Glenda Alcott
Mike Armijo
Brandon Bennett
Michael Bernstein
Ruth Berman
Linda Bowen
Connie Brooks
Doug Brotherton
Anne Burdick
Rodney Caro
David Carver
Caroline Cavella
Margo Chase
Eugene Cheltenham
Yee Ping Cho
Ken Coffelt
Karen Costello
Mandy Crespin
Joe D'Anna
Jim Deluise
Bruce Dizan
Richard Docter
James Duffin
Al Edwards
Anne Eichelberger

Ted Englebart
Kathy Fitzpatrick
Diane Foug
Laura Greunther
Vernon Hahn
Mark Harmel
Terry Irwin
Tamara Keith
Steve Kimura
Wendy Kramer
Sachi Kuwahara
Lisa Langhoff
Paul Langland
David Limwright
Michelle Lott
Robert Louey
Keith Macleod
Richard Maritzer
Kevin Mason
Mary Maurer
Victoria Miller
Marcia Mosko
Booker Rinder
Claudia Rossini
Regina Rubino
Judy Seckler

David Stern
Suzanne Tarbell
Mike Tuttle
Petrula Vrontikis
Donna Whitlin
Steve Wilbur

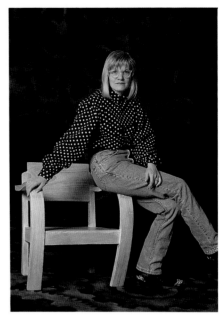

Jeri Heiden
Cover and Book Design

BOOK COMMITTEE
Linda Cobb
Kim Champagne
Christine Cano
Jeri Heiden
John Heiden
Melissa Hoel
Stuart Watson

This year's book, ADLA:5, is the fourth full-color, hard-bound volume of the Art Directors Club annual competition. A dedicated team of designers worked to compile the annual. Beginning with the format established for ADLA:2, the team moved on to scope out new territory, most significantly, adding a section devoted to the Lifetime Achievement Award recipient, Saul Bass.

The ADLA wishes to thank everyone who participated in the making of ADLA:5, from the art directors and designers who entered the competition to the judges who selected the work, and especially those people listed here.

Saul Bass
Lifetime Achievement
Award Recipient

Perhaps one of the most distinguished American designers alive, Saul Bass' influence has been felt as much in Main Street, U.S.A. as it has been in the design world. Anyone haunted by the famous shower sequence in "Psycho," for example, knows the power of Bass' work. The director of that segment, as well as the designer of countless familiar corporate symbols, commercial product packages and motion picture titles, this year's ADLA Lifetime Achievement Award winner is a man who has left an indelible mark not only on his colleagues, but on the collective consciousness of America as well.

Born in NYC, Bass began his career as a freelance graphic designer there in 1936. Ten years later he left for the West Coast, establishing Saul Bass & Associates, Inc., in Los Angeles in 1946. During these years and in the years to come, Bass designed and developed numerous trademarks and corporate identification symbols for such industrial giants as Bell System, AT&T, United Airlines, Alcoa, Quaker Oats, Rockwell International, Warner Communications, Minolta, Girl Scouts and United Way, among others. He also designed packages for commercial products like Wesson Oil, Dixie Paper, Lawry's Foods and others.

In the Fifties, Bass shared his talents for the first time with the film world, designing the graphic symbols for over sixty motion pictures, including such blockbusters as "Carmen Jones," 1954; "Bonjour Tristesse," 1956; "Anatomy Of A Murder," 1959; "Advise and Consent," 1962; "The Victors," 1964; "Seconds," 1966; and "The Shining," 1980. He also created over forty motion picture titles, including those for "Man With The Golden Arm," 1955; "North By Northwest," 1959; "Psycho," 1960; and "That's Entertainment: Part 2," 1974.

Not surprisingly, Bass' involvement in film gave him the itch to direct. Besides the shower sequence in "Psycho," Bass directed the final battle scene in "Spartacus," the live-action epilogue in "West Side Story" and other special sequences for numerous feature films.

But it was his work on short films which earned Bass the most acclaim as a director. His 1968 short, "Why Man Creates," won him an Oscar, an award for which he would be nominated again twice (in 1977 for "Notes On The Popular Arts," and in 1980 for "The Solar Film"). Other shorts earned him the Grand Award at the Venice Film Festival, the Gold Hugo at the Chicago Film Festival and the Gold Medal at the Moscow Film Festival, to name but a few.

Bass' entire body of work, in fact, has been honored in virtually every means possible. His films have been shown at retrospectives in Paris, Rotterdam and Zagreb. He is represented in the permanent collections of the Museum Of Modern Art in New York, the Library Of Congress and Smithsonian in Washington, D.C., the Prague Museum in Czechoslovakia and elsewhere throughout the world. A list of Bass' honorary degrees, medals and awards would fill pages of this book, as would an accounting of the many boards and faculties to which he has belonged. Suffice it to say that the ADLA Lifetime Achievement Award is but one of the many honors he has collected in his illustrious 50-year career.

Bass is married and the father of two children. He continues to design in Los Angeles at Saul Bass/Herb Yager & Associates.

Otto Preminger's

ANATOMY oF A MURDER

Starring James Stewart/Lee Remick/Ben Gazzara/Arthur O'Connell/Eve Arden/Kathryn Grant and
Joseph N. Welch as Judge Weaver/With George C. Scott/Orson Bean/Murray Hamilton/Brooks West.
Screenplay by Wendell Mayes/Photography by Sam Leavitt/Production designed by Boris Leven
Music by Duke Ellington/Produced and Directed by Otto Preminger/A Columbia release

CELANESE

PRIMO ANGELI
Principal
Primo Angeli Design

A student of Buckminister Fuller and Harold Cohen, Primo Angeli received a B.A. in Fine Arts and an M.S. in Communication from the University of Southern Illinois. He moved to California from his native Illinois in 1959 and established his own design firm, Primo Angeli Inc., in 1967.

Under Mr. Angeli's leadership, the firm has become one of America's leading marketing design companies, serving some of the world's most distinguished corporations. In providing corporate identity, packaging and environmental design for his clients, Mr. Angeli has received more than 400 national and international awards.

Recognition of Mr. Angeli's work include numerous CLIO Awards; Andy Awards for Excellence from the Advertising Club of New York; Gold and Silver Awards from the Art Directors Club of New York, the Western Art Directors Club, Package Design Council, Los Angeles Art Directors Club, and the San Francisco Society of Communicating Arts; and multiple awards for creativity from both *Communication Arts* and *Graphis.*

A number of Angeli designs are in permanent collections and exhibitions worldwide, including the Metropolitan Museum of Art, New York; Smithsonian Institution and Library of Congress, Washington D.C.; Cooper-Hewitt Museum of Design, New York; San Francisco Museum of Modern Art and the Achenbach Collection at the Legion of Honor Museum, San Francisco; the Centre Georges Pompidou and the Warsaw Poster Collections, Paris.

JEFFREY BACON
President
Bacon/O'Brien Design

It was 1:00 am at the Riverside Ramada Inn (sitting in on drums) that Jeffrey Bacon decided to be a graphic designer instead of a musician. Graduating from California State University at Fullerton, he formed his own design group in 1982. Specializing in movie posters, Jeffrey's clients include Warner Bros., Metro-Goldwyn-Mayer, Columbia, 20th Century Fox, Amblin Entertainment, Universal Pictures, Disney, and United Artists.

He is a former faculty member of Art Center College of Design and U.C.L.A. Extension. Jeffrey has received awards on his posters for "Back to the Future," "Rocky IV," "Ginger & Fred," and "Dreamgirls."

JIM BENEDICT
Art Director
Davis, Ball & Colombatto, Inc.

Jim Benedict's career in advertising began when he and his co-workers were instructed to come up with a name and advertising plan for a then-unknown popcorn snack. A short time later, this determined bunch of admen unleashed "Screaming Yellow Zonkers" upon the country, (the rest, of course, is snack history).

Looking for more excitement, Benedict exited hometown Chicago for New York. Spurning the ad agencies for the "freedom" of other endeavors, he somehow ended up working on a new product development at Spaulding and Leisure Dynamics by day while contributing to "Ladies and Gentlemen, The Rolling Stones" and "The Cher Show" at night.

Looking for less excitement he headed for Los Angeles where he somehow ended up opening a gallery and manufacturing business on a then-unknown street called Melrose. He gladly returned to the ad game in 1981.

Currently residing at Davis, Ball & Colombatto, Inc. Advertising, Jim Benedict is being held responsible for the "Mac Tonight" and "Tahiti Tourist Board" campaigns. Along the way, he managed to be named Adweek's "Television Art Director of the Year" on their All-Star Creative Team.

JIM BERTE
Principal/Design Director
Robert Miles Runyan & Associates

Born in the heartland of America in 1942 and again in 1947, Jim Berte developed an early interest in design. At the age of 3, his parents noticed that Jim had an aptitude for drawing in the dust during his breaks while working in the coal mines of Southern Kentucky. But his parents were hard working salt farmers who discouraged this frivolous behaviour. Years later, alone and hungry, Jim took the wallet from a helpless drunk. In it were admittance papers to the Rhode Island School of Design. Jim grasped gratefully at the life line, to graduate with honours in 1962 and again in 1964. After a brief career as a rodeo star and cowpuncher, Jim returned to his destined career of Design in St. Louis, Montreal and other Eastern cities.

Jim sought out the leading edge of design wherever he heard the call, carving out a reputation for himself in the process. While it has often been misquoted, Jim was the first to utter those now famous words "design is my life."

Gradually Jim's search for excellence and masculine restlessness brought him West. He joined the firm of Robert Miles Runyan & Associates. With him he brought the courage of his convictions, strength and on his brow sat wisdom. Within a few short years he brought the firm to national and international acclaim. Now, as a principal with the firm, Jim still brings innovation and insight to the most mundane of projects.

BRENT BOUCHEZ
Art Director
Ketchum Advertising

Brent Bouchez is Senior Vice President, Creative Director and Copywriter of Ketchum Advertising. Mr. Bouchez worked for Ogilvy & Mather, Chiat/Day, Inc. and Phillips-Ramsey before he began at Ketchum. Some of his clients throughout his career include Acura Automobiles, Pizza Hut, Yamaha Motor Corporation-USA, Porsche Cars North America, Mitsubishi Motors, Air California and San Diego Trust & Savings.

He has won many prestigious awards from the Clios, *Communication Arts,* The One Show, The Art Directors Club of New York, The Ad Club of New York and The Beldings.

LUCINDA COWELL
Creative Director
Concept Arts

Lucinda's career spans 20 years beginning with Lubalin and including her own studios in New York, London, San Francisco and North Hollywood.

She is currently founder and Creative Director of Concept Arts in North Hollywood, creating posters for independent movies such as, "Mona Lisa," "She's Gotta Have It," "True Stories" and "Sammy and Rosie Get Laid."

She has worked as an illustrator for Penguin, NAL, *Time Out,* Warner Bros. Records, *Mother Jones,* Simon & Schuster and the New Illustrators Show.

Her work as animation designer can be seen in "Monty Python's Holy Grail," and as a designer for Saul Zaentz' Fantasy Records and London's *Spare Rib* magazine.

GINA DAVIS
Art Director
Savvy Magazine

Gina Davis is a graduate of The City College of New York where she studied women's history. After a three year stint as a day care worker and union organizer she began her design career at Random House. There she was an apprentice to the art directors Louise Fili, Robert Scudellari and Susan Mitchell. Five years later she left to enter the world of magazines.

She is presently the art director of *Savvy* magazine, having worked at *Manhattan, Inc.* and *Esquire.*

BOB DEFRIN
VP/Creative Director
Atlantic Records

Born in New York City in the pre desk-top publishing era, he decided at an early age that he would never succeed at any worthwhile profession so he immediately started drawing. It didn't take long before he realized that he would never earn a living with illustration so he took the only road open to anyone with absolutely no drawing ability whatsoever. Graphic Design. At last, a way to earn money by tracing type and cropping photographs. Imagine, hiring others to do the hard work and then taking credit for their labors. He had found his niche.

Currently, he is Vice President and Creative Director of Graphics for Atlantic Records. He is the recipient of numerous awards from the Art Directors Clubs of L.A. and N.Y. (including a Gold Medal from the New York Club), the Type Directors Club, Society of Illustrators and AIGA.

He has four Grammy nominations for record album packaging and two posters in the permanent collection of The Museum of Modern Art.

He is a member of the National Academy of Recording Arts & Sciences, The Art Directors Club of N.Y., The Type Directors Club and the AIGA.

CAROL DeMELIO
Senior Art Director
Keye, Donna, Pearlstein

For a time, bad weather was Carol DeMelio's best friend.

She was born in New York during the blizzard of 19 (SFX door slamming/breaking glass).

Then, during the Boston blizzard of '78 which started after she finished art school, a small agency in a crunch (is there any other kind?) called and asked her to fill in. With pen frozen in hand, she managed to sled through the snow to start her career as an art director.

After a time, she discovered weather had nothing to do with her good fortune. So she went to Los Angeles where she worked at N.W. Ayer. Her accounts included the Australian Tourism Board and Yamaha musical instruments and sporting goods.

But she still had sixteen pair of winter boots in assorted colors to wear out. So, back to New York went Carol where she worked at Scali, McCabe, Sloves. There she worked on Nikon, Volvo and Continental Airlines.

Since the city did such a good job clearing the streets of snow there was nothing to ruin her boots. Once again, she moved. This time to someplace completely different, *West* L.A. She is currently at keye/donna/pearlstein working on the California Board of Tourism.

You can see her work in The One Show, CA, and The Art Directors Show.

NANCY DONALD
Senior Art Director
CBS Records

Nancy Donald is the Executive Art Director of CBS Records in LA. Born in NY, raised in LA, she's worked in the entertainment industry since her graduation from UCLA.

Her first job involved layout for a drag racing magazine where she designed pages with photos of upside-down carburetors. Following that, she became art director and photographer for a teen fan magazine where she exhibited greater facility handling photos of rock stars. She worked at Warner Bros. and as a free lance designer before joining CBS. Her work has been recognized by the AIGA, the Society of Illustrators, *Print* Magazine, *Graphis* and *IDEA* magazine, the ADLA and the New York Art Director's Club.

Nancy lives in LA with her son, a bunch of books and records, and two cats with flea problems.

PATRICK DOOLEY
Design Manager
J. Paul Getty Museum

Patrick Dooley is Design Manager for the J. Paul Getty Museum and The J. Paul Getty Trust Publications. As well as designing publications and installation graphics for the Museum, he oversees a broad range of materials produced for the programs of the Trust. Contrary to public impression, his main professional responsibility is not the spending of vast sums of money...he does, however, enjoy a priceless view of the Pacific Ocean from his office in a reconverted house behind the Museum in Malibu.

His publication work has won awards from the AIGA, New York Type Directors Club, Communication Arts, and the New York and Los Angeles Art Directors Clubs; he has also won awards for his work in educational interactive video.

Mr. Dooley is a graduate of the University of Iowa, where he studied painting and typography. He currently teaches at Otis/Parsons in Los Angeles and lives in a "transitional" neighborhood in Santa Monica with his wife Mary and daughter Claire.

RIP GEORGES
Art Director
Esquire

Considered by many to be one of America's premier magazine publication designers, Rip Georges has worked as an art director with *Revue, Arts & Architecture, LA Style,* and *Regardie's.* He has also served as art director and designer on projects as diverse as the Playboy Jazz Festival and 1978 Emmy magazine, in addition to co-authoring and designing *California Crazy* for Chronicle Books.

Georges has taught his craft at Art Center, Otis Parsons and U.C.L.A. Born in El Paso, Texas, he graduated from the University of California at Santa Barbara and received his postgraduate degree from Brighton College of Design in Sussex, England. He is currently Art Director at *Esquire.*

IVAN HORVATH
Creative Director
Ogilvy & Mather

DEBORAH GALLAGHER
Principal
Gallagher Design

JORDIN MENDELSOHN
Principal
Mendelsohn/Zien Advertising

Ivan Horvath came to the United States from his birthplace of Budapest, Hungary after he and his family fled the Hungarian Revolution in 1956.

He attended The School of Visual Arts (where he studied with Bob Giraldi, Clem McCarthy and Milton Glaser), Juilliard School of Music in New York and Ringling School of Art in Sarasota, Florida.

He started his ad career at Ogilvy & Mather in New York and worked there for 11 years as Producer/Art Director until he moved to Los Angeles for a position with NW Ayer, under the direction of John Littlewood. This was Ivan's first opportunity to function as a Creative Director in "the true sense of the title," he says.

After two long years with BBDO on Apple Computer and a stint with Jim Weller at Riney/LA, Ivan decided to go back to where it all began and took a job as Senior VP/Creative Director with Ogilvy & Mather.

Ivan has won several Clios, The Gold Lion (Cannes), the D&AD (London), the Belding Award, several One Show awards, honors from the Art Directors Clubs of NY and LA, Best in the West and the International Film and TV Festival.

Ivan also teaches advertising at Art Center College of Design in Pasadena. He already hired one great Art Director from his class and is about to hire another.

He spends his free time trying to play a Fender like Eric Clapton, piano like Keith Jarrett and photograph like Joel Meyerowitz or Maisel.

Deborah Gallagher lives and works in Minneapolis, Minnesota. She has worked for most, but not all, of the publishers there, designing airline inflight magazines, regional business magazines, and a city magazine. She was also the art director of PHOTO/DESIGN magazine from 1985 to 1988. Deborah started her own design firm in 1988.

Her work has won awards from AIGA/Minnesota, the International Association of Business Communicators, the Art Directors Club of New York and the Society of Publication Designers. She has also served as a judge for the Typographers International Association, the Art Directors Club of New York and the Society of Publication Designers.

Deborah is an active member of AIGA/Minnesota and currently serves as Vice President of that organization.

As a Los Angeles native and graduate of the Art Center College of Design in Pasadena, Jordin has worked as an Art Director for the past 12 years (Wells Rich Greene/Dentsu). He has created advertising for diverse clients including: fast food, automotive, fashion, packaged goods, toy, high-tech and financial companies.

He has won or been nominated for 43 major awards in all areas of television, print, outdoor and collateral, and his work has been recognized by every major U.S. advertising publication.

Jordin is currently teaching a course in "Advertising Concept" at UCLA and serves as Chairman of the Creative Committee for the Art Directors Club of Los Angeles.

JOHN MORRISON
Vice President / Senior Art Director
Levine, Huntley, Schmidt & Beaver

I've always been in the business. It's the only thing I know how to do. In the last five years I've worked at BBDO in L.A. on Apple Computer; Goodby, Berlin & Silverstein on Christian Brothers Brandy and the San Francisco Examiner; Chiat/Day, L.A. on Apple, mostly; and Fallon McElligott on AMF Heavyhands, Shade computer products and the 4A's. I'm well on my way to reaching one goal, which is to work for every agency in the country before I die. Also in the last five years I've won gold at Cannes, The One Show and New York Art Directors. I've gotten four Clios and five finalists into the Stephen E. Kelly Awards.

About judging I think Ed McCabe said it best: Too many of the people judging other people haven't reached any kind of pinnacle themselves. Still, given a choice between judging and being judged, I'd choose to judge.

MIKE MOSER
VP / Associate Creative Director
Chiat Day / San Francisco

After a start at Ramey Communications in Los Angeles, Mike moved to New York where he worked for Altschiller, Reitzfeld, Jackson & Solin. During his stay, ARJ&S was named hottest agency in the country under $25 million by *Adweek*.

In 1981, Mike moved to his current home at Chiat/ Day, where his creative work has made him one of the most recognized Art Directors in the country. His work for Apple, Businessland, Oral-B toothbrushes, California Cooler and Worlds of Wonder has earned him top honors in the Clios, the One Show and *Communication Arts*.

In 1983, Mike art directed three of the top ten magazine campaigns in the country (as noted by the Stephen E. Kelley Awards). He's also won five Clios and two bronze lions at the Cannes Film Festival since 1985.

He's been named the San Francisco Art Director of the Year—twice.

REX PETEET
Principal, Designer
Sibley-Peteet Design

Since 1975, after studying design at North Texas State University, Rex worked with several prestigious advertising and design firms including The Richards Group, Pirtle Design and Dennard Creative, prior to creating his own company with partner Don Sibley six years ago.

He has won numerous regional and national awards, including Dallas, Houston, Los Angeles and New York art directors shows. His work has been published frequently in *CA Magazine* and *New York Art Directors* Show annuals, as well as *Print, Graphis* and AIGA design annuals. His work is also represented in the permanent collection of the Library of Congress. In the 1985 New York Art Directors Club annual competition, Sibley/Peteet Design was the Southwest's top winner, receiving six major awards. Most recently, the firm was featured in the March/April issue of *Communication Arts* Magazine and the debut *HOW* Business Annual.

Rex is an active member in the Dallas Society of Visual Communications and is one of the founding members of the Texas chapter of the American Institute of Graphic Arts and serves on its board. Rex also judges, lectures and teaches seminars for various universities and art director/designer societies across the country.

"When not designing at work I'm designing at home, either landscaping or working around the house. I try and spend as much time as possible there with my wife, Gina, and two young daughters, Tara and Kate. If there's a moment left, I really enjoy playing guitar with friends from my band in college or snow skiing, but not at the same time."

DESIGN

ADVERTISING

LESLIE SMOLAN
Principal
Carbone Smolan Associates

Leslie Smolan has spent the past 12 years building one of the fastest rising design firms in New York City—Carbone Smolan Associates. Smolan, and her partner Kenneth Carbone, have intentionally kept their work broadly based, selling themselves as design generalists in a world of specialists. This formula has attracted major clients and projects internationally including the design of the bestselling "Day in the Life" book series, a line of dinnerware for Dansk International, signage programs for the Louvre in Paris, the Museum of Modern Art in New York, and the Los Angeles County Museum of Art, the corporate identity program for the American Stock Exchange, and marketing brochures for financial giant Merrill Lynch.

Smolan graduated from Philadelphia College of Art in 1975 with a BFA in graphic design. After graduation, she worked at Corporate Annual Reports for a year before returning to Philadelphia to teach typography and basic design at Philadelphia College of Art, and set up her own design firm. In 1977, she joined Kenneth Carbone in running the NY office of Gottschalk + Ash International. Carbone and Smolan completed one of the first leveraged buyouts of a design firm in 1980 and became Carbone Smolan Associates.

Her work has been published extensively in international magazines such as *Industrial Design, Graphis, Idea, Print, Communication Arts, Photo-Design, Step-by-Step Graphics, New York Woman, Working Woman, Life* and *Time.* She is currently on the board of the American Institute of Graphic Arts, on the advisory committee of *New York Woman* Magazine, and an active member of the Society of Typographic Arts (Chicago).

JEFFREY STARK
Creative Director
Saatchi & Saatchi / Compton

After several false starts as a barman, door to door salesman and a car salesman, Jeff Stark decided to work his way through Teacher Training College by becoming a bus conductor in his native Scotland. This ambition was thwarted when, not only did he fail to get in to college, he also failed the arithmetic test to be a bus conductor. He decided to embark on a career in advertising.

After a short spell as an assistant advertising manager in a store chain, he started as a copywriter in a small London advertising agency, mainly writing brochures on farm machinery, a subject about which he knew nothing. From there he moved to another unknown agency, now bankrupt, as a mail order copywriter. Here he sold muscle-building courses, patent zit removers and the kind of lingerie nice girls don't wear (another subject about which he knew nothing, but learned fast).

At the age of 28 he left to freelance. After 4 lucrative years of writing everything from jokes for men's magazine to books about plastic guttering, he became extremely bored. So he joined a small, relatively unknown advertising agency called Saatchi & Saatchi. He stayed there for seven years, winning several awards for his work on Schweppes, British Rail, the Youth Opportunities Programme, Leyland cars and British Caledonian Airways.

He then left Saatchi's to co-found his own London advertising agency, Hedger Mitchell Stark. This agency won many awards for its work on Olivetti, Fosters Lager and British Rail. Two years after starting, the agency was bought by Saatchi's and Jeff returned to Saatchi London, this time as Creative Director. After another two years, he moved to Saatchi DFS Compton in New York, where he still writes ads.

His ambition has always been to retire at the age of forty. He is now 44.

ELENA G. MILLIE
Curator of the Poster Collection
Library of Congress

THE ART DIRECTOR'S CLUB OF LOS ANGELES' 5TH
ANNUAL DESIGN COMPETITION HAS PROVIDED
AN IMPORTANT OPPORTUNITY FOR THE
LIBRARY OF CONGRESS TO ENHANCE ITS COL-
LECTION OF AMERICAN GRAPHIC DESIGN.

MS. ELEN'A G. MILLIE, A CURATOR FROM THE
LIBRARY'S PRINTS & PHOTOGRAPHS DIVISION,
SELECTED ENTRIES EXHIBITING IMPORTANT
CONTEMPORARY DESIGN TRENDS. THE COLLEC-
TION IS INTENDED FOR THE USE OF
RESEARCHERS INTERESTED IN THE HISTORY OF
GRAPHIC DESIGN. DESIGN IS A MIRROR OF THE
TIMES IN WHICH WE LIVE. DESIGN NOT ONLY
DOCUMENTS THE ICONS OF OUR TIME, BUT
ALSO REFLECTS CURRENT TECHNOLOGY. THE
ART DIRECTORS CLUB OF LOS ANGELES DOES A
TREMENDOUS JOB OF AMASSING THE BEST IN
GRAPHIC DESIGN FROM ACROSS THE COUNTRY.

Year after year, ADLA is supported by the generosity of many businesses. They contribute money, time, talent, creativity and moral support. Once again we thank all of them for their superb commitment to our organization and to our profession.

CONTRIBUTORS
Advertising Production Association
Albuquerque Budget Rent-A-Car
Albuquerque Convention & Visitors Bureau
Alpha Graphix
Anderson Lithograph
Anderson Printing
Andresen Typographics
Alan Barzman
Butler, Kosh & Brooks
ColorGraphics
El Dorado/Clarion Hotel
Sue Eck
Effective Graphics
Environmental Projection Systems
Gore Graphics
Graphis Type
G2 Graphics
Hopper Paper Company
Horn Graphics
Hollywood Typeset
Linda Lennon
Lennon and Associates
Los Angeles Advertising Women
Martin Brothers Winery
Gayle Miller
Molson Beer
Overland Printers
Paper Sources International
Polaroid Corporation
Prisma Color, Inc.
Reproduction Quality Services
Santa Fe Convention & Visitors Bureau
Snoqualmie Winery
Southwest Airlines
Tampico Tilly's
Typco Graphics, Inc.
Valenti Design
Warner Bros. Records
Stuart Watson Photography
J.B. West & Associates
Westland Graphics
West Light Stock Photography
Workbook
Zellerbach Paper Company

SPEAKERS

Joel Wayne
Warner Bros.

Alan Fletcher
Pentagram

Lou Dorfsman
CBS

Jeffrey Stark
Saatchi & Saatchi/Compton

Silas Rhodes
School of Visual Arts

Joe Duffy
The Duffy Design Group

Aaron Jones
Photographer

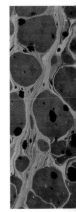

AWARDS

ART DIRECTOR
Bob Ribits
PRODUCERS
Angelo Antonucci
Carole Floodstrand
CREATIVE DIRECTOR
Gerry Miller
WRITER
Alex Goslar
CLIENT
Procter & Gamble / Cheer
AGENCY/STUDIO
Leo Burnett Company

"ICE CREAM"

AUDIO: Music throughout

"SOCKS"

AUDIO: Music throughout

"HANDKERCHIEF"

AUDIO: Music throughout

The Moving Finger writes; and, having writ,
Moves on: nor all thy Piety nor Wit
Shall lure it back to cancel half a Line,
Nor all thy Tears wash out a Word of it.

Omar Khayyám

ART DIRECTOR
Malcolm Waddell
DESIGNERS
Malcolm Waddell
Mercedes Rothwell
WRITERS
B.W. Power
George Houk
PHOTOGRAPHER
The Image Bank Canada
ILLUSTRATORS
Jan Waddell
Kate Waddell
CLIENT
Mead Paper
Empress Graphics Inc.
AGENCY/STUDIO
Eskind Waddell
▲

ART DIRECTOR
Matthew Drace
DESIGNER
Matthew Drace
PHOTOGRAPHER
Geof Kern
AGENCY/STUDIO
San Francisco Focus

  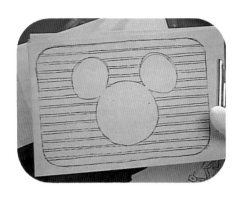

 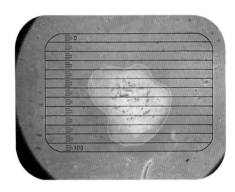 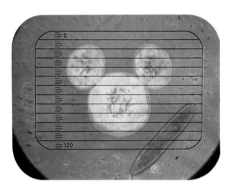

"MICKEY COUNTDOWN"

AUDIO: Music and sound effects throughout

"MICKEY FLIPBOOK"

AUDIO: Music and sound effects throughout

"MICKEY MICROSCOPE"

AUDIO: Music and sound effects throughout

ART DIRECTORS
George Evelyn
Carl Willat
DESIGNER
Mike Nichols
PRODUCER
Chris Whitney
DIRECTORS
George Evelyn
Carl Willat
WRITERS
George Evelyn
Don Smith
Carl Willat
PHOTOGRAPHER
Don Smith
CLIENT
The Disney Channel
AGENCY/STUDIO
Direct
PRODUCTION COMPANY
Colossal Pictures

ART DIRECTORS
Amy Nathan
Kathryn Kleinman

DESIGNER
Jacqueline Jones

FOOD STYLIST
Amy Nathan

WRITER
Jo Mancuso

PHOTOGRAPHER
Kathryn Kleinman

CALLIGRAPHER
William Stewart

CLIENT
Chronicle Books

AGENCY/STUDIO
Jacqueline Jones Design

ART DIRECTOR
Bill Cahan

DESIGNER
Cathy Locke

WRITER
David Crane

PHOTOGRAPHER
Burton Pritzker

ILLUSTRATOR
David Gambale

CLIENT
Babcock & Brown

AGENCY/STUDIO
Cahan & Associates

PRINTER
Lithographix
▲

ART DIRECTOR
Ken White

DESIGNER
Lisa Levin

WRITER
Aileen Farnan Antonier

PHOTOGRAPHERS
Eric Myer
Stan Klimek
Scott Morgan
Jeff Corwin
Terry Heffernan
Jayme Odgers
Burton Pritzker

ILLUSTRATORS
Bruce Dean
Don Weller

CLIENT
White & Associates

AGENCY/STUDIO
White & Associates

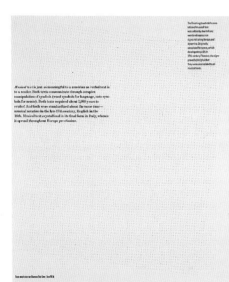

ART DIRECTOR
Gary Hinsche
DESIGNER
Michael Mescall
WRITER
William Wilson Co.
PHOTOGRAPHER
Norman Mauskopf
CLIENT
William Wilson Co.
AGENCY/STUDIO
Robert Miles Runyan
& Associates

ART DIRECTOR
Robert Appleton
DESIGNER
Robert Appleton
WRITER
Tom Mann
PHOTOGRAPHER
Various
ILLUSTRATOR
Various
CLIENT
Champion International
AGENCY/STUDIO
Appleton Design Inc.
▲

ART DIRECTORS
David Edelstein
Nancy Edelstein
Lanny French
DESIGNERS
David Edelstein
Nancy Edelstein
Lanny French
Sunny Shender
PRODUCER
D. Thom Bissett
WRITER
Kathy Cain
PHOTOGRAPHER
Barbara Penoyar
CLIENT
Generra Sportswear
AGENCY/STUDIO
Edelstein Associates
▲

ART DIRECTOR
Thomas Devine

DESIGNER
Thomas Devine

WRITERS
Victor Gill
Deborah Cohen

PHOTOGRAPHER
Scott Morgan

ILLUSTRATOR
Stephen Turk

CLIENT
Burbank Airport
Authority

AGENCY/STUDIO
Devine Design

DESIGNER
John Van Dyke

PHOTOGRAPHER
Terry Heffernan

CLIENT
Mead Paper

AGENCY/STUDIO
Samata Design

ART DIRECTOR
Jim Berté

DESIGNER
Jim Berté

WRITER
Julie Suhr

PHOTOGRAPHER
Scott Morgan

CLIENT
Nichols Institute

AGENCY/STUDIO
Robert Miles Runyan
& Associates

MAKING NEWS

MERIDIAN SL-100 GIVES TIME INC. THE POWER TO COMMUNICATE.

America's appetite for information is insatiable. World and national news. Sports. Pop culture. Business and finance. Tips on raising children. Ideas for home entertainment. We want to know it all. And one company—Time Inc.—has been satisfying this need to know longer and more completely than many news organizations in the United States.

Sixty-four years ago, the company published the nation's first newsmagazine, *Time*. It followed with *Life*, the icon of photojournalism, now in its 51st year of publication. Today, Time Inc. reaches 100 million readers with a portfolio of 37 magazines, among them *Sports Illustrated*, *People*, *McCall's*, *Fortune*, *Parenting* and *Southern Living*. Add Home Box Office (HBO) and Cinemax cable television, Time-Life Books, Book-of-the-Month Club and various other enterprises to its list of activities, and you get an even broader picture of the impact Time Inc. wields in informing, entertaining and influencing our society.

Headquartered in the Time & Life Building in New York City, Time Inc. is a tower of information. The 47-story building at Rockefeller Center is where the communication network is managed and where news from around the globe is filed, written, edited and published. The magazines are printed in plants throughout the US.

THE POWER TO COMMUNICATE

With so many Americans—and legions of foreign subscribers—relying on Time Inc. for quick and accurate communications, it is imperative that the company itself maintain quick and accurate communications within the organization and with the outside world.

Much of Time Inc.'s power to communicate comes from a new telecommunications system at its New York headquarters—Northern Telecom's Meridian SL-100 integrated services network. (Four of the company's regional offices are equipped with smaller Meridian SL-1s.)

After two years of extensive collaboration between Time Inc.'s communications department and Northern Telecom, the installation of the SL-100 in the Time & Life Building was completed in January 1987. Says Assistant Communications Manager Frank Fertura, "Northern Telecom was very good during installation. They worked very well with the additional contractors. When you're dealing with six or seven different types of trades, problems do come up." Currently the system is equipped with 4,500 phones and wired for 8,000.

With the SL-100, the corporation has a system it may never outgrow. The SL-100 has a capacity for up to 30,000 lines, but "there is no way we would ever get 30,000 lines in this building," says Bob Vernier, Time Inc.'s director of communications. He adds that everything is in place—a reliable and powerful switch, fiber optics cable, environmental specs—to handle as much growth as the building can accommodate.

Time Inc.'s magazine and book are imaginatively used in creation of television-oriented [illegible].

Axelrod Cavalier

First City Industries Inc.

JAMES F. HEINZ — H.J. HEINZ COMPANY LTD.

The most important change in the markets, the popular press tells Britain, is the return of the "good old competitive buyers' market." Well, the good old competitive spirit has returned, but in food it is anything except "the good old market."

To come at once to the most arresting point about Heinz U.K.: its productivity, performance and competitiveness the company is unique in the food industry. Indeed, it has few, if any, counterparts anywhere in British industry. Without undue fanfare at all, we have transformed the oldest overseas unit of Heinz into an advanced organization, where every employee is a highly capitalized, highly productive, highly motivated team member with the outlook of an aggressive entrepreneur.

Three years ago, it was clear that Heinz U.K. was running full speed into the most challenging era of its existence. Discounting by six national retail chains and cooperatives, each possessing its own growing private label, had become a permanent condition. For Heinz this meant not only a loss of bargaining power with its biggest customers, but a threat to the clear-cut character, prestige and reputation of its brands. The company was in danger of dropping into a position of secondary importance.

By contrast, Britain's food retailers act and think, in terms of units. A chain's management judges its performance and charts its future in terms of units and constantly alters for higher unit sales. So powerful is the assault from retailers that the private label has led out some fixed processors unable to break with the past.

In 1985, the largest single capital appropriation in company history was necessary to finance the transformation of every Heinz U.K. function. Large and small structural alterations in manufacturing, distribution and marketing were put into place. Every system and process was reshaped. To integrate the whole business into a finely tuned system, we make heavy use of computers and automation.

In the short run, we needed enormous improvements in productivity to meet the assault of private labels. In the long run, we needed to protect the competitive strength of our major brands—beans, soup, ketchup, pasta, baby foods and salad dressings. Some facts and figures show that the £100 million solution is working to revolutionary fashion.

Productivity, measured in tons per employee, is up almost 70% or so the past five years. Investment in technology has enabled us to reduce the number of employees from 5,800 in 1983 to 2,300. At the same time, we have increased or stabilized the market share of our volume lines, while aiming to increase the company's overall gross margins.

The sum total of progress in Britain in just three years is that we have an existing springboard into any facet of a "lowest cost imaginable" program. The people who are transforming Heinz tend to be young, unabashedly brainy, ambitious and aggressive. Nothing here there is—neither a rigid organization structure nor time-honored operating practices. They are building our future.

A cavalier is he who spent some years in Pittsburgh as vice president and controller of Heinz U.S.A., John E. Hitch is now managing director of Heinz U.K.

J. Heinz

ART DIRECTOR
Bryan L. Peterson

DESIGNER
Bryan L. Peterson

WRITER
Marsha Coburn

PHOTOGRAPHER
Geof Kern

CLIENT
Northern Telecom/
Barbara Wooley

AGENCY/STUDIO
Peterson & Company

ART DIRECTOR
Ron Jefferies

DESIGNER
Thomas Devine

WRITER
Nelson Fitch

ILLUSTRATORS
Tim Clark
Victor Hugo Zayas

CLIENT
First City Industries Inc.

AGENCY/STUDIO
The Jefferies Association

ART DIRECTOR
Bennett Robinson

DESIGNERS
Bennett Robinson
Erika Siegal

WRITERS
Jack Kennedy
Tom O'Hanlon

PHOTOGRAPHER
Rodney Smith

CLIENT
HJ Heinz Company

AGENCY/STUDIO
Corporate Graphics

ART DIRECTOR
Rex Peteet
DESIGNER
Rex Peteet
WRITERS
Mary Langridge
Rex Peteet
ILLUSTRATOR
Various
CLIENT
International Paper
AGENCY/STUDIO
Sibley/Peteet Design
▲

ART DIRECTOR
Doug Renfro
DESIGNER
Tim Frame
WRITER
Suzanne Harper
PHOTOGRAPHER
E.J. Camp
ILLUSTRATOR
Various
AGENCY/STUDIO
Whittle
Communications
▲

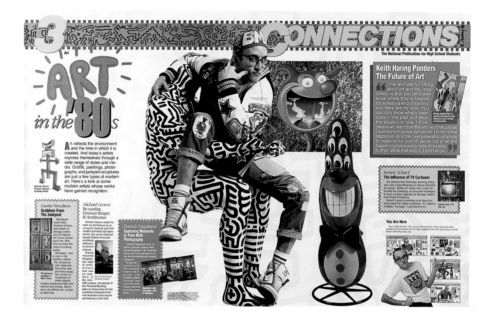

ART DIRECTOR
Wayne Hunt
DESIGNER
Brian Deputy
CLIENT
Kasparians, Inc.
AGENCY/STUDIO
Wayne Hunt Design

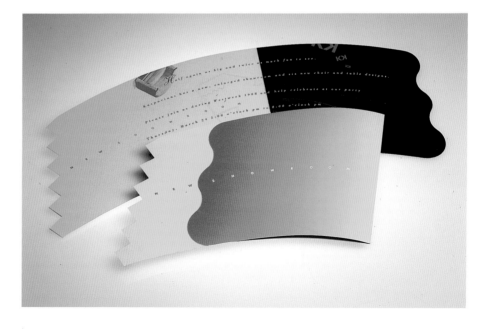

ART DIRECTOR
Cheryl Heller
DESIGNERS
Cheryl Heller
David Lopes
WRITER
Peter Caroline
PHOTOGRAPHER
Bruce Wolf
CLIENT
S. D. Warren
AGENCY/STUDIO
Heller Breene

ART DIRECTOR
Cheryl Heller
DESIGNERS
Cheryl Heller
David Lopes
WRITER
Peter Caroline
PHOTOGRAPHER
Lauri Rubin
CLIENT
S. D. Warren
AGENCY/STUDIO
Heller Breene

ART DIRECTORS
David Edelstein
Nancy Edelstein
Lanny French
DESIGNERS
David Edelstein
Nancy Edelstein
Lanny French
Sunny Shender
PRODUCER
D. Thom Bissett
WRITER
Kathy Cain
PHOTOGRAPHER
William Duke
CLIENT
Generra Sportswear
AGENCY/STUDIO
Edelstein Associates
▲

ART DIRECTOR
Siegfried Gesk
DESIGNER
Susan Strong
WRITER
Don Nesbitt
PHOTOGRAPHER
Hans Rott /
Shigeta & Associates
CLIENT
Austrian Oblaten Co.
AGENCY/STUDIO
Pedersen & Gesk, Inc.

ART DIRECTOR
Siegfried Gesk
DESIGNER
Kris Morgan
WRITER
Don Nesbitt
PHOTOGRAPHER
Hans Rott
Shigeta & Associates
CLIENT
Austrian Oblaten Co.
AGENCY/STUDIO
Pedersen & Gesk, Inc.

ART DIRECTORS
Koji Takei
Dennis Michael Dimos
DESIGNER
Koji Takei
CLIENT
JOICO Laboratories
AGENCY/STUDIO
Gormley/Takei, Inc.

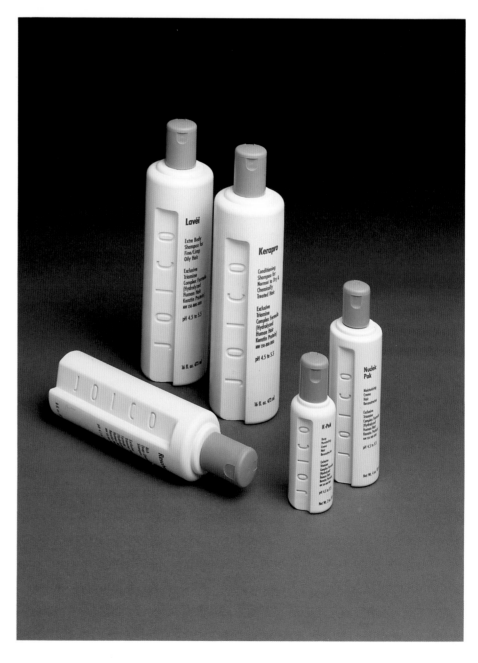

ART DIRECTOR
Rex Peteet
DESIGNER
Rex Peteet
ILLUSTRATOR
Sibley / Peteet Design
CLIENT
Dallas Museum of Art
AGENCY/STUDIO
Sibley / Peteet Design

ART DIRECTOR
Primo Angeli
DESIGNER
Ray Honda
PHOTOGRAPHER
Ming Louie
CLIENT
Shaklee Corporation
AGENCY/STUDIO
Primo Angeli Inc.

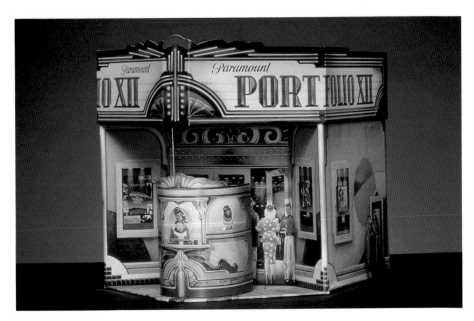

ART DIRECTORS
Randy Hipke
Brad Jansen
DESIGNERS
Randy Hipke
Brad Jansen
Keith Kaminski
ILLUSTRATOR
David MacMacken
CLIENT
Meryl Cohen
Paramount Pictures Corp.
AGENCY/STUDIO
5 Penguins, Inc.

ART DIRECTOR
Jon Reeder
DESIGNER
Lee & Porter Design
PRODUCER
Karen Garnett
WRITER
Rob Siltanen
PHOTOGRAPHER
Paul Taylor
ILLUSTRATOR
Richard Maritzer
CLIENT
Apple Computer Inc.
AGENCY/STUDIO
BBDO LA

ART DIRECTOR
Ivan Horvath
PRODUCER
Karen Garnett
WRITER
Ken Segall
PHOTOGRAPHER
Mike Chesser
CLIENT
Apple Computer Inc.
AGENCY/STUDIO
BBDO LA

ART DIRECTOR
Kathy Aird
PRODUCER
Karen Garnett
WRITER
Laurie Brandalise
PHOTOGRAPHER
Terry Hefernan
CLIENT
Apple Computer Inc.
AGENCY/STUDIO
BBDO LA

ART DIRECTOR
Richard Silverstein
WRITER
David Fowler
PHOTOGRAPHER
Marc Hauser
CLIENT
CA Magazine
AGENCY/STUDIO
Goodby, Berlin
& Silverstein

Tom McElligott's Son.

The One Show is the one show every Tom, Dick, and Harry dreams of getting into. For entry information, write The One Club at 3 West 18th Street, New York, New York, 10011. Or call 212-255-7070.

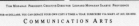

"**Lingerie reveals more of a woman than just skin.** When a woman wears beautiful lingerie it says she likes herself. I think that's sexy. To me, lingerie expresses how she feels. Playful. Romantic. Mysterious. The possibilities are always interesting."
  Maidenform offers women over 150 ways to express themselves. Obviously, people are listening.

M A I D E N F O R M

"**Lingerie says a lot about a woman. I listen as often as possible.** Lingerie doesn't cover a woman's body so much as uncover her personality. It tells me how she feels about herself. It also tells me how she feels about me…if I get to see it."
  Maidenform offers women over 150 ways to express themselves. And obviously, people are listening.

M A I D E N F O R M

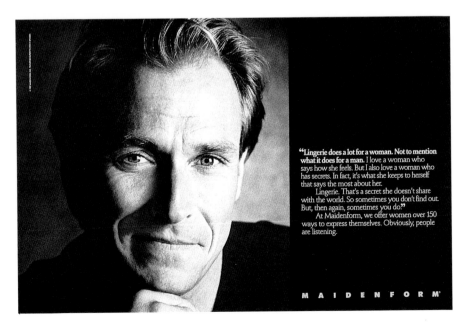

"**Lingerie does a lot for a woman. Not to mention what it does for a man.** I love a woman who says how she feels. But I also love a woman who has secrets. In fact, it's what she keeps to herself that says the most about her.
  Lingerie. That's a secret she doesn't share with the world. So sometimes you don't find out. But, then again, sometimes you do."
  At Maidenform, we offer women over 150 ways to express themselves. Obviously, people are listening.

M A I D E N F O R M

ART DIRECTORS
Tod Seisser
Irv Klein
WRITERS
Jay Taub
Stephanie Arnold
PHOTOGRAPHER
Henry Sandbank
CLIENT
Maidenform
AGENCY/STUDIO
Levine, Huntley
Schmidt & Beaver

ART DIRECTOR
Caball Harris
PRODUCER
Gary Beac
WRITERS
Daniel Russ
Mike Hughes (Blah-Blah)
PHOTOGRAPHER
Jim Erickson
(Tomato & Eggs)
CLIENT
Barnett Banks, Inc.
AGENCY/STUDIO
The Martin Agency

BUY AN ACURA. BECAUSE NOW BMW AND MERCEDES-BENZ STAND BEHIND IT.

A Number Of Our Conventions Have Lost Visitors To Sharks.

It happens every year. Driven by a desire to see all our fair city has to offer, but limited by time, large numbers of conventioneers slip away from seminars and speeches and head off seeking adventure.

Some fall prey to the sharks at the Shedd Aquarium.

Others to the lightning-quick snow leopards at the Lincoln Park Zoo.

And still others to the Museum of Natural History's giant dinosaurs.

Why, we've even heard tell of three men from Iowa who were lost to a 35-ft. boa constrictor at the Brookfield Zoo.

Obviously, we have a very serious problem on our hands. But fortunately, there's a simple solution.

Conventioneers visiting Chicago should just book a few extra days onto the beginning or end of their trip.

That way, they'll be able to attend their many meetings and still have time to indulge their wanderlust.

Whether they care to walk among the shops and boutiques of Michigan Avenue, the Picassos and Rembrandts of the Art Institute, or the sunbathers and windsurfers on our many beaches.

With proper planning they may even have time to take a boat ride along our shoreline. Or to view Chicago (plus Michigan, Wisconsin and Indiana) from atop the 1454-ft. Sears Tower.

Of course, there will no doubt be those who don't heed our advice. Who don't feel they need a few extra days to see our city.

Well, to them we offer this warning: the sharks are waiting.

For more information on Chicago, and all it offers, simply call us collect at (312) 567-8500.

Or send a telex to 312-433-0306.

Chicago Convention & Visitors Bureau

ART DIRECTOR
Jordin Mendelsohn

WRITER
Perrin Lam

CLIENT
Southern California
Acura Dealers

AGENCY/STUDIO
Mendelsohn/Zien

ART DIRECTOR
Brian Kelly

WRITER
Jim Schmidt

PHOTOGRAPHERS
Sharks:
Gwendolyn Cates

Museums & Restaurants:
Dave Jordano

CLIENT
Chicago Convention &
Visitors Bureau

AGENCY/STUDIO
McConnaughy
Barocci Brown

Claude Monet
Charing Cross Bridge
London
1901, oil on canvas
65.4 x 92.4 cm
The Art Institute
of Chicago

Claude Monet
Waterloo Bridge
1903, oil on canvas
65.7 x 101 cm
The Art Institute
of Chicago

The very same taxi ride will also take you to a Parisian Park (courtesy of Georges Seurat). A Tahitian Beach (courtesy of Paul Gauguin). And even a farm in the Midwest (courtesy of Grant Wood).

For those works of art—as well as numerous others from such folks as Picasso, Rembrandt, Toulouse-Lautrec, Degas and Van Gogh—are all part of the permanent collection at the

reach a point of museum ad nauseam, we'll simply say that you could spend a week in Chicago and still not see every dinosaur or ancient Egyptian urn we have to offer.

What about some less cultural pursuits, you ask?

Well, between our restaurants, shops, nightclubs, sports teams and lakefront you could also spend a week in our fair city and never even have

In Chicago, You Can Take A Taxi To Two Of London's Most Famous Bridges.

Art Institute of Chicago.

The Institute is just one of the many museums that make Chicago such a popular destination for convention and trade show visitors.

There's also the Field Museum of Natural History. The Museum of Contemporary Art. The Terra Museum of American Art. The Express-Ways Children's Museum. And the Museum of Science and Industry.

We could go on. But before we

time to look at a dinosaur or ancient Egyptian urn.

For more information on the many pleasures and entertainments we have to offer our convention and trade show visitors (as well as all the fine facilities we have to offer conventions and trade shows), simply call us collect at (312) 567-8500. Or telex us at 312-433-0306.

Our taxis will be standing by. **Chicago** Convention & Visitors Bureau

ART DIRECTOR
Brian Kelly

WRITER
Jim Schmidt

PHOTOGRAPHERS
Sharks:
Gwendolyn Cates

Museums & Restaurants:
Dave Jordano

CLIENT
Chicago Convention &
Visitors Bureau

AGENCY/STUDIO
McConnaughy
Barocci Brown

The lobster at the Cape Cod Room.

La Tarte aux Poires at Le Français.

The filet at Morton's

The bock beer at Berghoff's.

Some Of Our Most Enduring Attractions Disappear In Minutes.

The deep-dish pizza at Uno's.

The cheeseburger at Billy Goat's.

In the case of the full-bodied beer seen above, it's often only a matter of seconds.

But whether it's seconds or minutes, our point is simply this: when meeting in Chicago, be prepared for culinary temptation of the highest order.

Here, for example, one can literally take one's stomach on an epicurean tour of the world.

With stops in such exotic locations as Brazil. Ethiopia. Morocco. And Thailand.

Here, one can enjoy the delicate nuances of nouvelle cuisine one evening and the not-so-subtle pleasures of

a spicy meatball sandwich the next.

Here, one can dine under the stars (at any number of outdoor cafes), under the covers (courtesy of room service at any of our first-class hotels) and under the lights (at either of our major league ball parks).

Here, in short, one can satisfy one's appetite in just about any way imaginable.

For more information on Chicago, just call us collect at (312) 567-8500. Or telex us at 433-0306.

Temptation, on a grand scale, awaits. **Chicago** Convention & Visitors Bureau

The saganakki at Greek Islands (OOPAH!)

ART DIRECTOR
Brian Kelly

WRITER
Jim Schmidt

PHOTOGRAPHERS
Sharks:
Gwendolyn Cates

Museums & Restaurants:
Dave Jordano

CLIENT
Chicago Convention &
Visitors Bureau

AGENCY/STUDIO
McConnaughy
Barocci Brown

ART DIRECTOR
Yvonne Smith
PRODUCER
Karen Garnett
WRITER
Robert Chandler
CLIENT
Northrop Corp.
AGENCY/STUDIO
BBDO LA

WE CAN'T SHOW YOU WHAT WE'RE DOING, **BUT WE CAN SHOW YOU WHAT WE'VE DONE.**

We cannot display it, or diagram it, or illustrate it.

Nor are we publishing any photographs. And even when it flies, it will be virtually undetectable.

The Advanced Tactical Fighter.

F-23 prototypes being built for the Air Force by Northrop and McDonnell Douglas represent our forty years of experience building combat aircraft.

And, in fact, we have more fighter experience between us than any other

manufacturers in the free world today.

A heritage of thousands of frontline fighters. Including the F-4, the F-5, the F-15. And the F/A-18, the product of our ten year partnership. When deployed, the F-23 will deliver the decisive

edge. Where the enemy has both superior numbers and technological parity, it is the edge that will be essential if we are to prevail.

ATF-23
The Northrop/McDonnell Douglas Team

ART DIRECTOR
Michael Arola
DESIGNER
Michael Arola
CREATIVE DIRECTORS
Carolyn Johnson
Michael Arola
WRITER
Carolyn Johnson
PHOTOGRAPHER
Gastone Jung
CLIENT
Pirelli Tire Corp.
AGENCY/STUDIO
AC&R / CCL

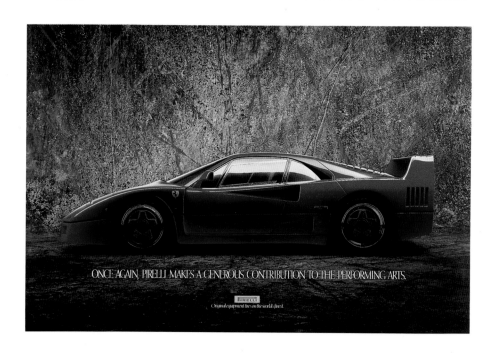

ONCE AGAIN, PIRELLI MAKES A GENEROUS CONTRIBUTION TO THE PERFORMING ARTS.

PIRELLI
Original equipment tires on the world's finest.

ART DIRECTOR
John Wagner
WRITER
Bill Day
CLIENT
WSAAA
AGENCY/STUDIO
Ogilvy & Mather

LISTEN CAREFULLY TO THIS CLASS AND YOU COULD END UP TEACHING IT.

Lee Clow
Chiat/Day

Tom Cordner
Ogilvy & Mather, L.A.

Paul Keye
keye/donna/pearlstein

Steve Hayden
BBDO/L.A.

Dan Wieden
Wieden & Kennedy

Brent Bouchez
Ogilvy & Mather, L.A.

Pacy Markman
DDB Needham Worldwide

Gary D. Johns
Johns+Gorman Films

Norman Berry
Ogilvy & Mather, N.Y.

Stephen Cunliffe
Cornerstone

Larry Postaer
Rubin Postaer & Assoc.

Jeff B. Gorman
Johns+Gorman Films

On October 28th, the WSAAA Carson & Roberts creative course will begin again for the fifth time. A rare advertising class taught by a rare group of advertising people.

Now all we need is a rare group of

advertising students. The best.

People cut from the same cloth as the ones you see here. With the same determination. The same passion. The same "Good enough is not enough" attitude. Not to mention the unique

ability to accept frank criticism or glowing praise with equal amounts of poise.

If this sounds like you, send us a sample of your work by October 19, 1987. If we like it, we really like it,

we'll call. Or, for more information, call Ruth Oreck: (213) 387-7432.

The WSAAA Carson & Roberts creative course. We'll teach you a lesson you'll never forget.

THE 5TH WSAAA CARSON & ROBERTS CREATIVE COURSE

Mail samples to WSAAA, 2001 Beverly Blvd., Suite 1, Los Angeles, CA 90057.

Most people who buy economy cars are missing a few screws.

ART DIRECTOR
Pam Cunningham
WRITER
Steve Bassett
PHOTOGRAPHERS
Diane Padys
Jon Kubly
CLIENT
Nissan Motor Corp
AGENCY / STUDIO
Chiat / Day

GENUINE MERCEDES REPLACEMENT PART.

ACURA
Southern California Dealers

ART DIRECTOR
Jordin Mendelsohn
WRITERS
Jordin Mendelsohn
Laurie Brandalise
CLIENT
Southern California
Acura Dealers

ACURAS DON'T CRUMPLE IN A CRASH LIKE OTHER LUXURY CARS DO.

ACURA
Southern California Dealers

BUY AN ACURA. BECAUSE NOW BMW AND MERCEDES-BENZ STAND BEHIND IT.

ACURA
Southern California Dealers

ART DIRECTOR
Jordin Mendelsohn
WRITER
Laurie Brandalise
PHOTOGRAPHER
Jay Ahrend
CLIENT
Southern California
Acura Dealers

ART DIRECTOR
Jordin Mendelsohn
WRITER
Perrin Lam
CLIENT
Southern California
Acura Dealers

ART DIRECTOR
Jordin Mendelsohn
WRITER
Jordin Mendelsohn
CLIENT
Southern California
Acura Dealers
AGENCY/STUDIO
Mendelsohn/Zien

ART DIRECTOR
Jordin Mendelsohn
WRITERS
Jordin Mendelsohn
Laurie Brandalise
CLIENT
Southern California
Acura Dealers
AGENCY/STUDIO
Mendelsohn/Zien

ART DIRECTOR
Richard Crispo
WRITER
Scott Aal
PHOTOGRAPHER
Bo Hylen
CLIENT
American Honda Motor
Co., Acura Division
AGENCY/STUDIO
Ketchum Advertising

"FRIENDS"

V.O. You're looking at a car with the highest level of owner satisfaction ever recorded…It's an Acura…Statistics show that an incredible 99.1 percent of Acura owners would recommend their car to a friend…What about the other point nine percent?…Maybe they just have a hard time getting hold of their friends.

Acura. Cars for people who know better.

Priced from 10 to 29 thousand dollars.

ART DIRECTOR
Tom McManus

PRODUCERS
Ed Pollack
Susan Jurick

DIRECTORS
Alan Charles
Bert Dubois

WRITER
David Warren

CLIENT
Tri-State Acura Dealers

AGENCY/STUDIO
TBWA Advertising Inc.

PRODUCTION COMPANY
Charles St. Films,
DuBois Films

ACURA

CARS FOR PEOPLE WHO KNOW BETTER.

ART DIRECTOR
Tom McManus

PRODUCERS
Ed Pollack
Susan Jurick

DIRECTORS
Alan Charles
Bert Dubois

WRITER
David Warren

CLIENT
Tri-State Acura Dealers

AGENCY/STUDIO
TBWA Advertising Inc.

PRODUCTION COMPANY
Charles St. Films,
DuBois Films

"BULLHORN"

DRIVER 1: (HIS VOICE IS AMPLIFIED OVER A BULLHORN) I am a young urban professional ...Look at my $42,000 Mercedes...Aren't you impressed?

ANNCR: At Acura, we think the way to impress people is not by showing how much money you spent on your car...but by showing how much car you got for your money.

DRIVER 2: (HIS VOICE IS ALSO AMPLIFIED) I am a very successful young urban professional ...Look at my BMW...Am I not beautiful?

ANNCR: Acura. Cars for people who know better. Priced from 10 to 29 thousand dollars.

ACURA

**CARS FOR PEOPLE
WHO KNOW BETTER.**

"NO MERCEDES"

V.O. Presenting the Acura Legend coupe...And the Mercedes 560...Auto World magazine compared these two cars for ride, acceleration, fit and finish...A total of fourteen categories...The Acura finished dead even with the Mercedes... The only difference between the two cars? The price...The Mercedes costs more than twice as much as the Acura...That's why you don't see the Mercedes here...We couldn't afford one for this commercial.

Acura. Cars for people who know better.

ART DIRECTOR
Tom McManus

PRODUCERS
Ed Pollack
Susan Jurick

DIRECTORS
Alan Charles
Bert Dubois

WRITER
David Warren

CLIENT
Tri-State Acura Dealers

AGENCY/STUDIO
TBWA Advertising Inc.

PRODUCTION COMPANY
Charles St. Films,
DuBois Films

ART DIRECTOR
Tim Boxell
DESIGNER
Michael Nichols
PRODUCER
Chris Whitney
DIRECTOR
Tim Boxell
WRITER
Tim Boxell
PHOTOGRAPHER
Bob Dalva
CLIENT
The Disney Channel
AGENCY/STUDIO
Direct
PRODUCTION COMPANY
Colossal Pictures

"MICKEY'S MOTORBOAT"

AUDIO: Music and sound effects throughout

 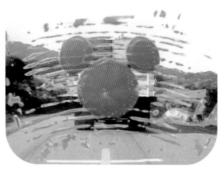

"MICKEY'S ROAD SIGN"

AUDIO: Music and sound effects throughout

ART DIRECTOR
Carl Willat
DESIGNER
Michael Nichols
PRODUCER
Chris Whitney
DIRECTOR
Carl Willat
WRITER
Carl Willat
PHOTOGRAPHERS
Bob Dalva
Steven Lighthill
ANIMATION
Carl Willat
Scott Tolmie
CLIENT
The Disney Channel /
Robin Steele
AGENCY/STUDIO
Direct
PRODUCTION COMPANY
Colossal Pictures

ART DIRECTOR
Carl Willat

DESIGNER
Michael Nichols

PRODUCER
Chris Whitney

DIRECTOR
Carl Willat

WRITER
Carl Willat

PHOTOGRAPHERS
Bob Dalva
Steven Lighthill

ANIMATION
Carl Willat
Scott Tolmie

CLIENT·
The Disney Channel /
Robin Steele

AGENCY/STUDIO
Direct

PRODUCTION COMPANY
Colossal Pictures

"MICKEY'S MILKBOTTLE TOSS"

AUDIO: Music and sound effects throughout

"MICKEY'S NIGHTMARE"

AUDIO: Music and sound effects throughout

ART DIRECTOR
Carl Willat

DESIGNER
Michael Nichols

PRODUCER
Chris Whitney

DIRECTOR
Carl Willat

WRITER
Carl Willat

PHOTOGRAPHERS
Bob Dalva
Steven Lighthill

ANIMATION
Carl Willat
Scott Tolmie

CLIENT
The Disney Channel/
Robin Steele

AGENCY/STUDIO
Direct

PRODUCTION COMPANY
Colossal Pictures

ADVERTISING

NEWSPAPER

ART DIRECTOR
Tom Cordner

WRITER
Brent Bouchez

PHOTOGRAPHER
David Leach

CLIENT
California Federal

AGENCY/STUDIO
Ogilvy & Mather

ART DIRECTOR
Keith Evans

DESIGNER
Keith Evans

WRITER
Ken Shuldman

PHOTOGRAPHER
Bruno

CLIENT
Cigna

AGENCY/STUDIO
DDB Needham
Worldwide

ART DIRECTOR
Jerry Torchia

PRODUCER
Wayne Woods

WRITER
Luke Sullivan

PHOTOGRAPHER
Museum Staff
Photographer

CLIENT
Henry Ford Museum/
Greenfield Village

AGENCY/STUDIO
The Martin Agency

Spot remover.

Find good homes for Spot, Fido and Rover by advertising in the Herald Examiner Classified Section. Or you can bring home a brand new pooch for yourself. Three lines for seven days costs only fifteen dollars.* Call (213) 744-8100 or 1-800-252-9393. MasterCard and Visa gladly accepted.

*Private Party Rate

What to do if the Rabbit dies.

Don't panic, just buy another car through the Herald Examiner Classified Section. It's a great vehicle for finding the one you want. And for selling the one you don't. Three lines for seven days, only fifteen dollars.* Call (213) 744-8100 or 1-800-252-9393. MasterCard and Visa gladly accepted.

*Private Party Rate

NEWSPAPER

ART DIRECTOR
Richard Crispo
WRITER
Scott Aal
PHOTOGRAPHER
Michael Justice
CLIENT
American Honda Motor
Co., Acura Division
AGENCY/STUDIO
Ketchum Advertising

ART DIRECTOR
Richard Crispo
WRITER
Scott Aal
PHOTOGRAPHER
Michael Justice
CLIENT
American Honda Motor
Co., Acura Division
AGENCY/STUDIO
Ketchum Advertising

ST. MARY'S IS NOW CARING FOR WOMEN IN TWENTY DIFFERENT LOCATIONS.

Since the day St. Mary's opened its doors in 1966, our doctors and nurses have been providing women with the most thorough health care available. No matter how small their needs. Or how large.

Which is why you'll find anyone from an expectant mother to a 95-year-old grandmother taking advantage of our facilities and programs.

Like our NewLife Center. Where maternity patients and their families are finding birth more memorable due to a dedicated staff and the great benefits of St. Mary's Little Lamb Club.

We also have a Women's Imaging Center with mammography for the early detection of breast cancer, as well as ultrasound and a number of other diagnostic x-ray procedures.

Then there's sports medicine. Weight control. Same day surgery. Wellness and fitness. A lending library of books and videos on women's health. Plus seminars on just about everything you can imagine from nutrition to family life.

In fact, there are so many good things going on for women at St. Mary's we can't possibly fit them all in this ad. So if you want more information just call our referral coordinator at 673-LADY. Or feel free to stop by the hospital at 5801 Bresee Road.

The location we're known for best.

✝ ST. MARY'S HOSPITAL

ART DIRECTOR
Diane Tench
DESIGNER
Diane Tench
PRODUCER
Meredith Ott
WRITER
Liz Paradise
PHOTOGRAPHER
Richard Ustinich
CLIENT
St. Mary's Hospital
AGENCY/STUDIO
The Martin Agency

TARGET MARKETING IS LIKE DIVING 75 FEET INTO A BUCKET OF WATER.

You don't want to miss.

Because, in target marketing, aim is everything.

You have to reach the people who can buy what you have to sell.

Which is why, if your target is business or the affluent, there's just one place to aim.

The Wall Street Journal.

Every business day, we reach 6.2 million people with the power to say "Yes." And with the affluence and influence to turn "Yes" into sales.

Our subscribers have an average household income of $107,800. And an average household net worth of nearly $800,000.

Among those in business and the professions, over half hold top management positions. With the authority to initiate and approve major purchases.

That makes The Journal's audience the perfect target for marketers of everything from computers and convention sites to luxury homes and cars.

And if you're targeting one part of the country?

In addition to Journal editions, we now offer Southern California and Southeastern Regions. So you can target your advertising to two of the fastest growing economic areas in the world.

No matter which editions or regions you select, you'll reach those who can say the one word every marketer wants to hear. "Yes."

The Wall Street Journal.

Where target marketers make a big splash.

THE WALL STREET JOURNAL

IT WORKS.

ART DIRECTOR
Petter Thoen
WRITER
Doug Johnston
PHOTOGRAPHERS
Craig Saruwatari
Gil Smith & Co.
CLIENT
The Wall Street Journal
AGENCY/STUDIO
Gil Smith & Co.

NEWSPAPER

ART DIRECTOR
Cabell Harris

PRODUCER
Gary Beach

WRITER
Daniel Russ

PHOTOGRAPHER
Cosby/Bowyer

CLIENT
Barnett Banks, Inc.

AGENCY/STUDIO
The Martin Agency

ART DIRECTOR
Steve Luker

PRODUCER
Deborah Wieland

WRITER
Alan Yamamoto

PHOTOGRAPHER
Dale Windham

CLIENT
Brown & Haley

AGENCY/STUDIO
McCann-Erickson

ACURAS DON'T CRUMPLE IN A CRASH LIKE OTHER LUXURY CARS DO.

When the stock market took a big dive last October, sales of European luxury cars weren't very far behind.

According to the November 5th edition of the Los Angeles Times, Mercedes-Benz reported that sales in the month of October '87 were down 25.7% from the year before. BMW said that its sales fell off 10.5%. And Porsche cited a full 30% drop.

It seems that almost all of the high priced luxury cars lost a bit of their allure after the October crash. In fact, one out of three Americans polled said they planned to postpone or reduce major purchases, such as an automobile.

Yet in spite of this cautionary spending trend, one luxury import seemed to fare quite well. Instead of declining sales, it posted October gains of 40.3% from the year before.

That car was the Acura.

Of course, this isn't to say Acura buyers aren't careful with their money. On the contrary. At around twenty-two thousand dollars, the Acura Legend is perhaps the most rational luxury car purchase one can make.

Both Car and Driver and Road & Track Magazines have named it one of the ten best cars in the world.

And the most recent J.D. Power Customer Satisfaction Index, a survey of twenty thousand new car owners, puts Acura ahead of Mercedes by a substantial nineteen percentage points. And ahead of BMW by a whopping forty points.

Which just goes to prove that crash or no crash, you can feel very safe in an Acura.

ACURA
Southern California Dealers

TWO OF THE TOP THREE LUXURY CARS IN THE COUNTRY HAVE TERRIBLE SLIPPAGE PROBLEMS.

A curious thing happened to Mercedes and BMWs recently. They've started slipping.

But this slippage has nothing to do with either automobile's excellent transmission or anti-lock brake system. Which is somewhat unfortunate. Because those problems can be easily fixed.

The slippage problem were referring to is more complicated. And is caused by something a lot more serious.

A decline in customer satisfaction.

You see, it all started with this year's highly respected J.D. Power Customer Satisfaction Index. What the J.D. Power survey does is ask a lot of questions. Of lots of drivers.

Questions like: How many problems has your car had while under warranty? How many times has it needed fixing after it was

fixed the first time? And were there even parts to fix it with?

After reading through all the responses, there emerged a very clear picture of what...

**1987 J.D. POWER
CUSTOMER SATISFACTION INDEX**

...it's like to own a Mercedes. A BMW. And an Acura.

But something else emerged, too. Mercedes-Benz wasn't on top of the list. No, not this year. This year, Mercedes slipped to an unprecedented third place.

And BMW, an embarrassing eleventh.

The car that came in first, by 19 percentage points better than Mercedes and a whopping 40 points better than BMW, was the Acura Legend.

Which should really come as no surprise. After all, since its introduction in '86, Acura has been compared equal to or better than both Mercedes and BMWs on numerous occasions. Why this year alone, it won Motor Trend's import car of the year award.

So if you're thinking of buying a Mercedes or a BMW, think again. You could be making a major slip-up.

ACURA
Southern California Dealers

NEWSPAPER

ART DIRECTOR
Jordin Mendelsohn
WRITER
Laurie Brandalise
PHOTOGRAPHER
Jay Ahrend
CLIENT
Southern California
Acura Dealers
AGENCY/STUDIO
Mendelsohn/Zien

ART DIRECTOR
Jordin Mendelsohn
WRITER
Perrin Lam
PHOTOGRAPHER
Jay Ahrend
CLIENT
Southern California
Acura Dealers
AGENCY/STUDIO
Mendelsohn/Zien

ART DIRECTOR
Steve Luker
PRODUCER
Deborah Wieland
WRITER
Alan Yamamoto
PHOTOGRAPHER
Dale Windham
CLIENT
Brown & Haley
AGENCY/STUDIO
McCann-Erickson

THEY'RE ONLY UGLY UNTIL YOU TASTE THEM.

Brown & Haley Mountain® Bars.

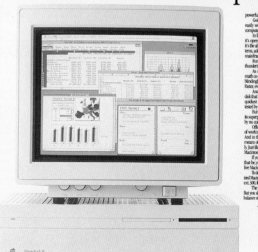

"HONEY, I'M HOME."

The homeless. Who are they? Bums? Mental patients? Tramps? People who wouldn't know a home if they saw one?

Guess again. One-third of L.A.'s homeless population is made up of families. Mothers. Fathers. Children. The homeless group that's growing the fastest. Families like yours and ours. Families that perhaps were once your neighbors.

Families that would like to be your neighbors again.

We're building a better Los Angeles. That's our name. Our community is your community. Our goal is your goal. Our target this year is to raise several million dollars. If you love L.A., you'll help us build a better L.A.

Think about it when you get home tonight.

BUILDING A BETTER LOS ANGELES

A non-profit corporation • 8383 Wilshire Boulevard, Suite 700 • Beverly Hills, CA 90211 • 213/655-7330
Co-Chairmen: Supervisor Michael D. Antonovich • Mayor Tom Bradley • Nathan Shapell

7:42 AM, October 1, 1987

When the shaking stopped, our people moved heaven and earth.

As soon as they got out from under their desks, the people at GTEL's 24-hour Trouble Analysis Center got on their phones.

Checking the thousands of California customers who depend on GTEL—rain, shine or earthquake—for their business communications.

Not that they had to test every line personally. Our computer is programmed to test most major systems remotely and at high speed. (It's something we do routinely to make sure everything's functioning as it should.)

After the quake, we found five business systems that were off-line.

And we were able to reach our service technicians in the affected areas before they even left home. (That's one benefit of having a fleet of more than 450 fully equipped vans statewide.)

The result was that as our customers were arriving for the start of a day's business, most of GTEL's technicians were already leaving.

With the systems back on-line.

This kind of service comes at no extra charge when you select GTEL for your communications needs.

And if you call for information on a PBX system by June 6, 1988, so does something else.

A free $2,000 service package.

We're giving away our remote diagnostic service package with every qualifying PBX system. It's valued at up to $2,000, and helps to reduce downtime in your system by identifying problems as soon as they occur.

Call Michael Fontaine at 1-800-657-5323 and he'll fill you in on the details of this special offer.

You'll discover that when you become a GTEL customer, we do our very best to make sure of one thing.

That there are no after-shocks for you.

GTEL
GTE

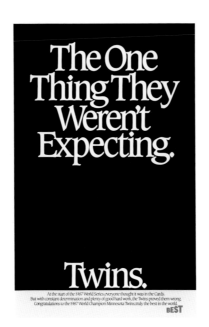

The One Thing They Weren't Expecting.

Twins.

At the start of the 1987 World Series, everyone thought it was in the Cards. But with constant determination and plenty of good hard work, the Twins proved them wrong. Congratulations to the 1987 World Champion Minnesota Twins, truly the best in the world.

BEST

NEWSPAPER
ART DIRECTOR
Wayne Gibson
PRODUCER
Meredith Ott
WRITER
Luke Sullivan
PHOTOGRAPHER
Alex Pacheco
CLIENT
People for the Ethical
Treatment of Animals
AGENCY/STUDIO
The Martin Agency

Imagine having your body left to science while you're still in it.

Three animals die every second in U.S. laboratories.

The monkey pictured here was surgically crippled and then forced to use his deadened arm.

Other animals, including rabbits, dogs, and cats are routinely blinded, shocked, mutilated, decapitated and force-fed poisons in tests which could easily be replaced with modern and more reliable alternative tests.

These sadistic animal tests are being conducted by the government, universities, medical associations, and profit-making corporations.

And always behind closed, locked doors. Pigs, rats, chickens, horses and other laboratory animals suffer by the millions.

The cost to U.S. taxpayers, however, is in the billions.

If you think these kinds of cruel experiments have no place in the 20th century, please join us: People for the Ethical Treatment of Animals.

PETA is America's leading animal rights organization. By working with medical and legal professionals, the media, members of Congress, and people like you, PETA has been able to stop some of the most horrifying animal experiments, including the one pictured here.

Even as you read this ad, there are thousands more lab experiments being conducted without your knowledge, *but with your tax dollars.*

So please join us today.

People For The Ethical Treatment Of Animals

ART DIRECTOR
Wayne Gibson
PRODUCER
Meredith Ott
WRITER
Luke Sullivan
PHOTOGRAPHER
Alex Pacheco
CLIENT
People for the Ethical
Treatment of Animals
AGENCY/STUDIO
The Martin Agency

ART DIRECTOR
Wayne Gibson
PRODUCER
Meredith Ott
WRITER
Luke Sullivan
PHOTOGRAPHER
Alex Pacheco
CLIENT
PETA-People for the
Ethical Treatment
of Animals
AGENCY/STUDIO
The Martin Agency

If you liked pulling the wings off flies as a kid, you may be cut out for a career in animal experimentation.

People For The Ethical Treatment Of Animals

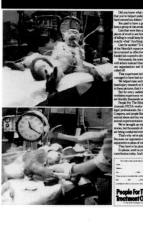

Thanks to a $12 million government grant, scientists have conclusive proof that monkeys die when their skulls are crushed.

People For The Ethical Treatment Of Animals

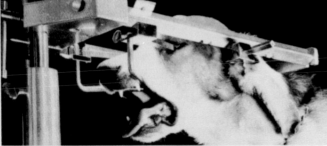

People For The Ethical Treatment Of Animals

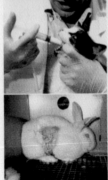

NEWSPAPER

ART DIRECTOR
Wayne Gibson

PRODUCER
Meredith Ott

WRITER
Luke Sullivan

PHOTOGRAPHER
Alex Pacheco

CLIENT
People for the Ethical
Treatment of Animals

AGENCY/STUDIO
The Martin Agency

ART DIRECTOR
Wayne Gibson

PRODUCER
Meredith Ott

WRITER
Luke Sullivan

PHOTOGRAPHER
Alex Pacheco

CLIENT
People for the Ethical
Treatment of Animals

AGENCY/STUDIO
The Martin Agency

NEWSPAPER

ART DIRECTOR
Bill Maddox
WRITER
Bob Sundland
PHOTOGRAPHER
D.J. Hawkins
CLIENT
San Diego Zoo
AGENCY/STUDIO
Phillips Ramsey

C25-55

ART DIRECTOR
Kevin McCarthy
DESIGNER
Kevin McCarthy
WRITER
Chris Thompson
PHOTOGRAPHER
Marshall Harrington
CLIENT
San Diego County
Toyota Dealers
AGENCY/STUDIO
Phillips-Ramsey
PRODUCTION COMPANY
Kathy Kevern

ART DIRECTOR
Chip Kettering
DESIGNER
Chip Kettering
WRITER
Vicki Grondyke-Nichols
ILLUSTRATOR
Jeff George
CLIENT
Vons Grocery
Companies Inc.
AGENCY/STUDIO
J. Walter Thompson

The Zoo's latest attraction was captured in the waters off Australia.

This Saturday only, see the America's Cup at the San Diego Zoo. View the trophy won by San Diego's own "Stars & Stripes." You don't have to be a member of the San Diego Yacht Club to see the Cup on Saturday. You just have to be in the Zoo.

The most famous prize in yachting will be on display from 9 a.m. to 4 p.m. for one day only, January 30th, by arrangement with the San Diego Yacht Club. If you're here for the Super Bowl, you ought to see the Super Cup. **The San Diego Zoo**

Our Mechanics Learn How To Fix Cars With Tape.

The wonders of videotape. It's an ideal medium for communicating important information. And our Toyota Service Technicians view tapes like these as part of their Continuing Education. It's their idea of Educational Television. What our Service Techs learn from this process helps them improve how they care for

your Toyota. What's become known as Toyota Loving Care. This kind of TLC you'll only find at your San Diego County Toyota Dealers. And you'll only find it here because the kinds of television programs that we watch, all have the same happy ending. A better cared for Toyota, for you.

San Diego County Toyota Dealers.

Put some foreign objects in your mouth this weekend.

Come to Tianguis' SampleFiesta and taste chorizos, empanadas, ceviche, machaca, calabacitas and all sorts of things Mom never used to make. **TIANGUIS**

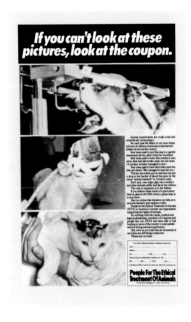

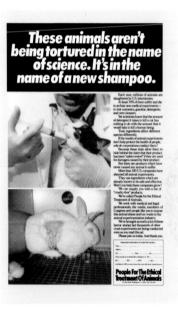

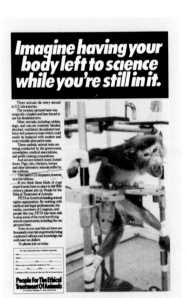

NEWSPAPER
CAMPAIGN

ART DIRECTOR
Wayne Gibson

PRODUCER
Meredith Ott

WRITER
Luke Sullivan

PHOTOGRAPHER
Alex Pacheco

CLIENT
People for the Ethical
Treatment of Animals

AGENCY/STUDIO
The Martin Agency

ADVERTISING

NEWSPAPER
CAMPAIGN

ART DIRECTOR
Richard Crispo

WRITER
Scott Aal

PHOTOGRAPHER
Michael Justice

CLIENT
American Honda Motor
Co., Acura Division

AGENCY/STUDIO
Ketchum Advertising

Spot remover.

Find good homes for Spot, Fido and Rover by advertising in the Herald Examiner Classified Section. Or you can bring home a brand new pooch for yourself. Three lines for seven days costs only fifteen dollars.* Call (213) 744-8100 or 1-800-252-9393. MasterCard and Visa gladly accepted.

What to do if the Rabbit dies.

Don't panic. Just buy another car through the Herald Examiner Classified Section. It's a great vehicle for finding the one you want. And for selling the one you don't. Three lines for seven days, only fifteen dollars.* Call (213) 744-8100 or 1-800-252-9393. MasterCard and Visa gladly accepted.

It's all over L.A.

Kiss your grandfather goodbye.

If it's gotta go, it's gotta go. The Herald Examiner Classified Section is great for selling clocks and all kinds of furniture. A great place to find them, too. Three lines for seven days, only fifteen dollars.* Call (213) 744-8100 or 1-800-252-9393. MasterCard and Visa gladly accepted.

*Private Party Rate

NEWSPAPER
CAMPAIGN

ART DIRECTOR
Wayne Gibson
PRODUCER
Chet Booth
WRITER
Andy Ellis
CLIENT
Richmond Boys Club
AGENCY/STUDIO
The Martin Agency

THE LIFEGUARDS AT THE BOYS CLUB KEEP A CLOSE WATCH. IN FACT, LAST YEAR THEY SPOTTED THREE CASES OF CHILD BEATING.

The Boys Clubs of Richmond boasts a staff of 21. We say "boasts" because we're proud of their ability to find the potential and talents that exist in each individual boy.

But perhaps prouder of those occasions when they've spotted the less obvious. Things like learning disabilities, emotional problems and even abuse.

If you'd like to support these efforts, call 359-5250 to learn how.

BOYS CLUBS OF RICHMOND

LIKE MANY FATHERS, JAMES' DAD SHOWED HIM HOW TO SHOOT A GUN. HE WAS COMMITTING SUICIDE AT THE TIME.

This is a true story we recently faced at the Boys Club. So, if you think this is just a place where kids go to play basketball, think again.

And remember that when you support the Boys Club, you're also encouraging things like cultural appreciation, health education, job training, and counseling for boys in need of emotional support.

To learn how you can support these efforts, call 359-5250.

BOYS CLUBS OF RICHMOND

AT AN AGE WHEN MOST BOYS ARE ASKING WHERE BABIES COME FROM, WE KNOW ONE 10 YEAR OLD WHO FEARS HE MIGHT HAVE GONORRHEA.

The purpose of this ad isn't to speculate why kids are becoming more "sophisticated."

It's to tell you the Boys Club recognizes this fact. And responds by educating.

So we've introduced kids to speakers from drug rehabilitation centers, Alcoholics Anonymous, Planned Parenthood and on and on.

To learn how you can support these efforts, call 359-5250.

BOYS CLUBS OF RICHMOND

NEWSPAPER
CAMPAIGN

ART DIRECTOR
Steve Stone
DESIGNER
Betsy Zimmermann
WRITER
David Fowler
PHOTOGRAPHER
Jay Maisel
CLIENT
Royal Viking Line
AGENCY/STUDIO
Goodby, Berlin
& Silverstein

RIO DE JANEIRO MONTREAL MAZATLAN ACAPULCO PANAMA CANAL BANGKOK SAN JUAN ST. THOMAS ANTIGUA GRENADA TRINIDAD DEVIL'S ISLAND TOKYO

On Our First Visit
To Midway Island, We Wish To Thank
Those Who Have Been Before.

China/The Orient:
> March 26: Hong Kong > Tokyo
Pacific Crossing:
> April 13: Tokyo > Los Angeles
> Air transportation included
> Free land packages

Ports of Call:
Hong Kong > Shanghai >
Beijing > Kobe >
Tokyo > Midway Islands >
Honolulu >
San Francisco >
Los Angeles

On April 18, by special permission of the U. S. Navy, the Royal Viking Sea will become the first cruise ship ever to visit Midway Island.

This maiden call occurs en route from Hong Kong, Beijing, and Tokyo to San Francisco and Los Angeles. Entertainers Victor Borge and Rita Moreno will make it a most pleasant crossing.

At Midway, Captain Ed Beach, naval historian and author of *Run Silent, Run Deep* will provide perspective on Midway's role as an early telegraph link; as a vital stopover for the famed China Clipper; and as the setting on June 4, 1942 for perhaps the most decisive air and sea battle in history.

Further particulars are available from your courteous travel agent, or by phoning (800) 872-8386. As always, we look forward to seeing you on board.

Most important of all, to the U. S. Navy and its members who made this visit possible, thank you.

ROYAL VIKING LINE

BOSTON SYDNEY HOBART MELBOURNE AUCKLAND WELLINGTON HONG KONG REYKJAVIK SHANGHAI BEIJING DALIAN INLAND SEA NAGASAKI LENINGRAD

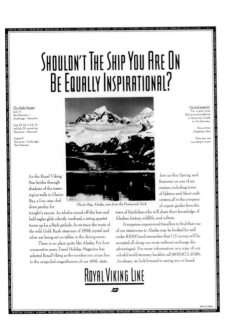

Shouldn't The Ship You Are On
Be Equally Inspirational?

As the Royal Viking Star knifes through shadows of the towering ice walls in Glacier Bay, a five-star chef dices parsley for tonight's sauces. As whales sound off the bow and bald eagles glide silently overhead, a string quartet tunes up for a Bach prelude. As we trace the route of the wild Gold Rush steamers of 1898, crystal and silver are being set on tables in the dining room.

There is no place quite like Alaska. For four consecutive years, Travel Holiday Magazine has selected Royal Viking as the number one cruise line to the unspoiled magnificence of our 49th state.

Join us this Spring and Summer on one of six cruises, including tours of Eskimo and Aleut craft centers, all in the company of expert guides from the town of Ketchikan who will share their knowledge of Alaskan history, wildlife, and culture.

It surprises experienced travellers to find that one of our staterooms to Alaska may be booked for well under $3000 (and remember that U.S. money will be accepted all along our route without exchange disadvantage). For more information or a copy of our colorful world itinerary booklet, call (800)872-8386. As always, we look forward to seeing you on board.

ROYAL VIKING LINE

ART DIRECTOR
Betsy Zimmermann
DESIGNER
Betsy Zimmermann
WRITER
Jeff Goodby
PHOTOGRAPHER
(Stock)
CLIENT
Royal Viking Line
AGENCY/STUDIO
Goodby, Berlin
& Silverstein

In Celebration Of
Going Nowhere, Slowly.

It is a feeling fast disappearing from the face of the earth—the ocean crossing, with its vaunted tranquility, camaraderie, and uncompromised elegance.

Very soon, the ships of Royal Viking will be making two of these rare passages, and you are invited to join us at a price that—with all land programs and air transportation fares—begins around $125 per day. (Experienced travellers will recognize that this is a rather extraordinary figure.)

Our Atlantic crossing departs April 10th, featuring land packages in Lisbon or Fort Lauderdale—and an optional stay in Madrid. The Transpacific trip includes two hotel nights in Tokyo, one in Kyoto, and two more in Honolulu.

Aboard ship, you will be regaled with the five-star cuisine, service, and entertainment you expect from Royal Viking. Omar Sharif, the celebrated actor and less celebrated but still dangerous bridge player, will join us on the Atlantic crossing to present and discuss his films. During the Pacific trip, Maxene Andrews of the Andrews Sisters will perform, lecture, and host a party.

For more information send a copy of our 1988 Welcome Aboard cruise atlas, please call (800) 872-8386. As always, we look forward to seeing you on the ship.

ROYAL VIKING LINE

ART DIRECTOR
Betsy Zimmermann
DESIGNER
Rich Silverstein
WRITER
Jeff Goodby
CLIENT
Royal Viking Line
AGENCY/STUDIO
Goodby, Berlin &
Silverstein

MAGAZINE
ART DIRECTOR
Tracy Wong
DESIGNER
Tracy Wong
WRITER
Mike La Monica
PHOTOGRAPHER
David Langley
CLIENT
Ogilvy & Mather
AGENCY/STUDIO
Shing Unlimited

ART DIRECTOR
Dennis Lim
WRITERS
Scott Aal
Brent Bouchez
CLIENT
Ketchum Advertising
AGENCY/STUDIO
Ketchum Advertising

ART DIRECTOR
Carlos Segura
DESIGNER
Carlos Segura
WRITER
Chuck Rudnick
CLIENT
Women's Ad Club
of Chicago
AGENCY/STUDIO
Zwiren & Partners

ART DIRECTOR
Rich Silverstein

WRITER
David Fowler

PHOTOGRAPHER
Marc Hauser

CLIENT
CA Magazine

AGENCY/STUDIO
Goodby, Berlin
& Silverstein

ART DIRECTOR
Rich Silverstein

WRITER
David Fowler

PHOTOGRAPHER
Marc Hauser

CLIENT
CA Magazine

AGENCY/STUDIO
Goodby, Berlin
& Silverstein

ART DIRECTOR
Rich Silverstein

WRITER
David Fowler

PHOTOGRAPHER
Marc Hauser

CLIENT
CA Magazine

AGENCY/STUDIO
Goodby, Berlin
& Silverstein

ART DIRECTOR
Rich Silverstein

WRITER
David Fowler

PHOTOGRAPHER
Marc Hauser

CLIENT
CA Magazine

AGENCY/STUDIO
Goodby, Berlin
& Silverstein

ART DIRECTOR
Rich Silverstein

WRITER
David Fowler

PHOTOGRAPHER
Marc Hauser

CLIENT
CA Magazine

AGENCY/STUDIO
Goodby, Berlin
& Silverstein

ART DIRECTOR
Rich Silverstein

WRITER
David Fowler

PHOTOGRAPHER
Marc Hauser

CLIENT
CA Magazine

AGENCY/STUDIO
Goodby, Berlin
& Silverstein

MAGAZINE

ART DIRECTOR
Charlie Clark

WRITER
Leslie Clark

PHOTOGRAPHER
Glen Silker

CLIENT
James A. Cassidy Co.

AGENCY/STUDIO
Susan Davis
Advertising Group

ART DIRECTOR
Tom Cordner

WRITER
Brent Bouchez

CLIENT
Ogilvy & Mather

AGENCY/STUDIO
Ogilvy & Mather

ART DIRECTOR
John Wagner

WRITER
Bill Day

CLIENT
Ogilvy & Mather

AGENCY/STUDIO
Ogilvy & Mather

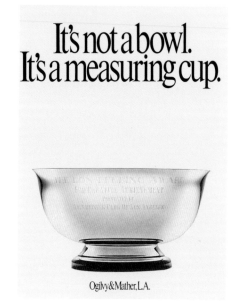

ART DIRECTOR
Aki Seki

DESIGNER
Aki Seki

WRITER
Michael Lichtman

CLIENT
Franklin Typographers

AGENCY/STUDIO
Workaholics Anonymous

ART DIRECTOR
Steve Beaumont

WRITER
Hillary Jordan

ILLUSTRATOR
Stéve Kimura

CLIENT
Ketchum Advertising

AGENCY/STUDIO
Ketchum Advertising

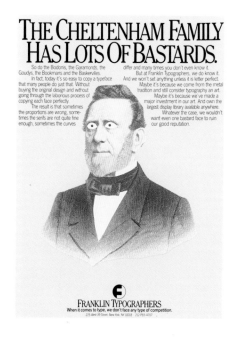

WHEN YOUR ROOF JUST HAS TO LAST.

A dependable roof is a way of life. It has to protect its owner from anything the elements can dish out; sun, chemicals, severe temperature swings, even acid rain. And look good doing it.

That's where Robertson comes in. With our Total Performance Roof. Protected by Versacor® PF. A coating system that combines our Versacor® epoxy base coat with a PPG Duranar® finish. And creates what is simply the most durable metal roof available.

What's more, the Versacor PF Coating System costs only about 15 cents more per square foot than most ordinary thin-film paints. So you can include it in your specs without running for cover.

Skeptical? We'll prove it. Just write H.H.Robertson Company, Department AR6, 400 Holiday Drive, Pittsburgh, PA 15220. Or call (412) 928-7500.

We'll send you a free copy of our Independent Test Results brochure. And show you how to get roofing problems off your back. Once and for all.

The No Compromise Roof

PPG   Robertson

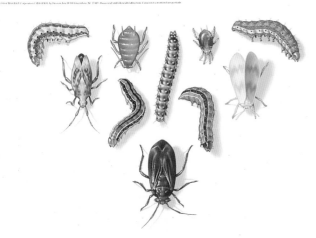

Curacron. The best broad-spectrum defense for cotton.

You can now prevent the worst pests from making a boll-bid all season long.

Because Curacron® offers early, mid, and late-season protection for your cotton plants. Broad-spectrum control for the entire season.

When hot weather brings early-season mite damage, Curacron provides the control you need.

Curacron's mid-season protection offers excellent broad-spectrum control. Especially when pressure comes from secondary pests like lygus, beet armyworm, and aphids. Budworm, bollworm, or leafperforator. And while Curacron may not give commercial control, it offers suppression of whitefly. Plus, Curacron can be used alone or in a tank mix to address specific insect problems.

And Curacron provides unsurpassed clean-up of late-season insects. At full rates.

All of which means no pests, and no problems. Throughout the season.

What's more, Curacron isn't affected by high or low temperatures—and is absorbed into the leaves to provide a lasting residual protection.

So make Curacron an integral part of your control program this season. And put the big ten where they belong. The end zone.

CIBA–GEIGY

HOW TO KEEP THE BIG TEN FROM MAKING IT TO THE COTTON BOLL.

BUILDERS QUALITY PLEDGE

WE'RE ADVERTISING SOMETHING NO ONE WILL EVER NEED.

Black & Decker is so confident in the quality of its Professional tools that our Builders Quality Pledge offers customers a full refund within 30 days of their purchase, if they're not satisfied.

But frankly, we don't think we'll have too many takers. Because when tools consistently perform the way they're supposed to, you don't end up with too many complaints.

The Builders Quality Pledge is just one way we're proving our commitment to your business.

In addition, we'll be bringing you new programs, promotions, and advertising in the months to come.

Black & Decker understands that the most important thing we can guarantee is customer satisfaction.

NOTHING BEATS A
BLACK & DECKER

MAGAZINE

ART DIRECTOR
Jon Reeder

PRODUCER
Karen Garnett

WRITER
Ken Segall

PHOTOGRAPHER
Paul Taylor

CLIENT
Yamaha Digital
Musical Instruments

The MIDI guitar has always looked like a good idea.

Now it sounds like one.

Guitarists now have the power to do something that's always been lingering in the back of their minds: Control the world.

Introducing the Yamaha® G10 Guitar MIDI Controller.

Combined with the rack-mount G10C Guitar MIDI Converter, it lets you drive almost any MIDI device you choose, be it a synthesizer, sampler, tone generator or drum machine.

But most important, the G10 system recognizes you for what you really are. A guitarist.

In fact, it lets you use every expressive trick of the trade. There's no frustrating delay. You can bend notes. Damp them. Even play pull-off and hammer-on notes.

You can instantly change styles, too. Because each of the 64 internal memories (and 64 cartridge memories) in the G10C contains a full set of performance parameters such as individual string volume, capo position, tuning and controller assignments. Any one of which can be called up at the touch of a button.

But you've waited long enough for a MIDI guitar that really works. So stop reading.

Call 800-333-4442 for an authorized Yamaha Digital Musical Instruments dealer and go play the G10 system. Without delay. **YAMAHA.**

ART DIRECTOR
Ken Sakoda

DESIGNER
Reyes Art Works

CREATIVE DIRECTORS
Scott Montgomery
Ken Sakoda

WRITER
Scott Montgomery

PHOTOGRAPHER
John Svoboda

CLIENT
Marcy

AGENCY/STUDIO
Reyes Art Works

ENGRAVER
Spectra

EVER WONDER WHY MOST PEOPLE MAKE LOVE IN THE DARK?

Come on, you know why.

It's because that one-piece suit nature gave us is far more revealing than baggy sweaters and old jeans.

But Marcy's here to tip the scales in your favor.

Marcy's been making fitness products for over 40 years.

Quality fitness products like the EM/1 you see pictured here. The home fitness center you can buy for a year's worth of dues at the typical gym.

You'll find a heavy duty leg station for powerful calves, quads and hamstrings.

Serious arm curl, lat and abdominal stations.

And a button-busting 320-pound bench capacity.

Fourteen stations in all.

All ruggedly built to last for years and years to come.

So check out the complete Marcy EM/1 series today.

Your body will improve. Your stamina will improve. Your energy will improve.

Not to mention the fact you'll start seeing your love life in a whole new light.

Call 1-800-62MARCY, ext. 17 for your nearest dealer.

MARCY
FITNESS PRODUCTS
WHEN YOU FINALLY GET SERIOUS.

What today's musicians could use is a good dose of reality.

For years now, Yamaha has been giving you the tools to explore new musical worlds.

But today we'd like to direct your attention to planet earth. Where you can capture sounds that are absolutely real, with the new TX16W Digital Wave Filtering Stereo Sampler.

The TX16W allows you to sample anything you can hear, and then filter that sound while it's still in digital form. So you can create the cleanest possible tonal effects.

It also gives you the power to experiment with a wide range of sounds only possible with stereo sampling.

Perhaps even more important, the TX16W lets you build sounds in a very realistic way. For example, you can assign up to 32 samples to any single voice, for a natural effect across the entire keyboard.

In addition, you can layer up to 16 voices, using the Crossfade function to assign designated voices to different sections of the keyboard. Resulting in gradual tonal changes, as opposed to abrupt splits.

Likewise, a Touch-Crossfade feature makes it possible for you to combine designated voices as a function of key velocity.

To give you an even more natural sound, the TX16W has 32 individual LFOs, one for each of the 32 timbres that can make up a single voice.

There's yet another LFO for each of the 32 digital filters. And for good measure, a global performance LFO.

Of course, in keeping with Yamaha tradition, the TX16W has a number of other features to make your musical life easier.

Like a built-in 3.5" disk drive that quickly saves or loads even complex setups. A 40 x 2 LCD you can read in most any kind of light. A numeric keypad for fast data entry.

As well as 1.5 megabytes of memory, which you can easily bump to six megabytes via plug-in modules.

And all this power in a package that takes up only two rack spaces.

If you'd like a sample of what the TX16W can do, stop in and see your nearest authorized Yamaha Digital Musical Instruments dealer.

We realize it may seem like too much sampler for the money, but that's the way it is.

Welcome to the real world.

⬥ YAMAHA

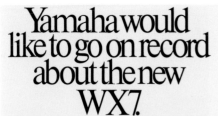

Yamaha would like to go on record about the new WX7.

After all these years, there's finally been a change in the winds.

Thanks to our new WX7 Wind MIDI Controller, reed players can now drive tone modules, synthesizers, drum machines—all the MIDI technology that Yamaha has developed over the years.

And the beauty of it is, if you play a woodwind instrument, you already know how to play a WX7.

Its 14 keys are light and responsive, and follow the traditional Boehm layout. They're also adjustable to suit your own playing technique.

But when it comes to controlling sound, the WX7 Wind MIDI Controller is anything but traditional.

For example, it lets you play over a

range of 7 octaves. Hold one note while you play another. And bend pitch effectively even in the lowest register.

With the WX7, it's actually easier to play trills than it is with a regular saxophone. Because you use the same whole-and half-note trill keys no matter what octave you're playing in.

It also has a sax-like mouthpiece that senses both breath and lip pressure. Which, with the right settings on your tone module, can be assigned to control such parameters as volume, tremolo, vibrato, tone and articulation.

All the expressive control that you demand as a woodwind player.

Of course, news of this magnitude is often hard to swallow.

So to help convince you, we're enlisting the aid of two of your most trusted friends. Your ears.

Just remove the attached sound-sheet and hear for yourself what our new controller can do.

As we said earlier, the WX7 Wind

MIDI Controller has brought about a real change in the winds.

We stand by that statement. In fact, now it's a matter of public record.

⬥ YAMAHA

The forecast is for incredible winds.

Tie down all loose objects.

With the WX7 Wind MIDI Controller, woodwind players everywhere will be playing up a storm.

Because now, they too can tap into the full range of powerful MIDI technology that Yamaha has developed over the years.

The WX7 can drive tone modules, synthesizers, even drum machines—and still give you the kind of control you demand as a reed player.

Its 14 fully-adjustable keys are arranged in a traditional Boehm layout, so you already know how to play it. But "traditional" is hardly the word to describe the things you can play.

For example, the WX7 makes it possible for you to play over a range of seven octaves. Hold one note while you play another. And bend pitch effec-

tively throughout the entire note range.

The WX7's mouthpiece is very much like that of a saxophone. And with the proper settings on your tone module, breath and lip pressure can control such parameters as volume, tremolo, vibrato, tone and articulation.

Two trill keys make it easy to perform half-and whole-note trills, using the same fingering in every register. While a Program Change Key lets you switch programs as you play.

And if all this sounds incredible here, just imagine how it sounds at an authorized Yamaha Digital Musical Instruments dealer.

So go try a WX7 for yourself. And brace yourself for some powerful winds.

⬥ YAMAHA

MAGAZINE

ART DIRECTOR
Julie Markell

WRITER
Brandy French

CLIENT
Conroy's Florists

AGENCY/STUDIO
J. Walter Thompson

Somewhere in this world there's a woman with pictures of you naked.
Be nice to her.

CONROY'S FLORISTS

ART DIRECTOR
Jan Kovaleski

DESIGNER
Karen Newe

WRITER
David Alverson

PHOTOGRAPHER
Amedeo Buhler

CLIENT
1928 Jewelry Company

AGENCY/STUDIO
Miles Communications

ART DIRECTOR
Richard Crispo

WRITER
Bob Ancona

PHOTOGRAPHER
Terry Heffernon

CLIENT
Security Pacific
Merchant Bank

AGENCY/STUDIO
Ketchum Advertising

Cheers to your ears!

1928
Jewelry Company

Money makes the world
go round. Making money go around
the world is another matter.

Security Pacific Merchant Bank

ART DIRECTOR
Kathryn Windley

DESIGNER
Kathryn Windley

WRITER
Brent Bouchez

PHOTOGRAPHER
Henry Bjoin

CLIENT
Carnation Pasta
& Cheese

AGENCY/STUDIO
Ogilvy & Mather

We've Refined The Art Of Making Fresh Pastas And Sauces Down To 86 Easy Steps.

You May Want To Skip 1 Through 83.

You'll find Contadina Fresh pastas and sauces in the
refrigerated section of your supermarket.

HE MAY NOT BE COVERED PROPERLY.

Suppose this statue had to be shipped to another location. What would happen if it was damaged in transit?

Chances are the insured would discover the statue was missing something very important. Namely, thousands of dollars in coverage.

Because while certain policies may protect your property while it's on your premises, after it leaves, it could be stripped of virtually all protection.

With property and casualty needs becoming increasingly complex, it's not surprising that businesses are often unaware of gaps in their insurance programs. Last year, American businesses let millions of dollars slip through those gaps. Which is why at CIGNA, we're constantly developing ways to reduce them.

One way is with our business package policy. An exceptional policy we invented and sell more of than anyone else. It enables us to tailor

specific coverages and build them around the needs of your business. Coverages designed to close gaps. Like our transportation coverage, which would guarantee payment for a loss, even when the shipper of the statue isn't liable.

Furthermore, at the CIGNA Companies, we offer an array of business insurance products rarely available from a single insurer. All backed by strong claims service, experienced loss control specialists and one of the most advanced computerized risk-information systems in the industry.

Without the proper coverage, you could expose yourself to numerous unnecessary risks. Call your CIGNA company agent, check your local listings or write CIGNA Companies, Dept. R16, 1600 Arch Street, Phila., PA 19103 and learn how we can help fill in the missing pieces of your program.

CIGNA

We spend all the time we're open getting ready to close.

About the only thing more impressive than California Federal's national capabilities is California Federal's local capabilities.

Partly because every Cal Fed® loan center in Florida and Georgia has the authority to originate, process, appraise, approve, generate documents and fund your client's loan.

Without leaving town.

Best of all, right now all of our loan centers are providing 10-day home loan funding, thanks to our streamlined local operations.

Which means you can expect to do a lot more closing, a lot more often.

Try us. Call us. Our computerized loan status network and our 24-hour pager system are open for business as you read.

But do hurry.

Because we can't wait to close.

CALIFORNIA FEDERAL
Well Managed Money.™

The one that coats
is the only one you need.

MAGAZINE

ART DIRECTOR
Keith Evans

DESIGNER
Keith Evans

WRITER
Ken Shuldman

PHOTOGRAPHER
Bruno

CLIENT
Cigna

AGENCY/STUDIO
DDB Needham
Worldwide

ART DIRECTOR
Kathryn Windley

DESIGNER
Kathryn Windley

WRITER
Greg Voornas

PHOTOGRAPHER
Michael Ruppert

CLIENT
California Federal

AGENCY/STUDIO
Ogilvy & Mather

ART DIRECTOR
Jeff Gregg

CREATIVE DIRECTOR
Dan Heagy

WRITER
Bob Welke

CLIENT
P&G / Pepto Bismol

AGENCY/STUDIO
Leo Burnett Company

MAGAZINE

ART DIRECTOR
Bryan Birch

PRODUCER
Karen Garnett

WRITER
Robert Chandler

CLIENT
Northrop Corp.

AGENCY/STUDIO
BBDO LA

ART DIRECTOR
Yvonne Smith

PRODUCER
Karen Garnett

WRITER
Robert Chandler

PHOTOGRAPHER
Jim Hall
Lamb & Hall

CLIENT
Northrop Corp.

AGENCY/STUDIO
BBDO LA

No one is affected by hunger as much as a child. Malnutrition often inflicts a healthy young body with diminished brain development. Rickets. Even blindness.

In Los Angeles, a large percentage of the 1.5 million people going hungry are children.

By collecting mostly unsaleable food that would otherwise go to waste, LIFE is feeding many of them.

With your donation, we could feed more. So please call us at (213) 936-5111. Because a problem this small can't be overlooked.

Hunger is just a small problem in L.A.

With Your Help We Can Sustain It.

To 1.5 million people in L.A. this is about as obtainable as a house in Beverly Hills.

LIFE
With Your Help We Can Sustain It.

MAGAZINE

ART DIRECTORS
John Armistead
John Fisher
WRITER
Rick Lester
PHOTOGRAPHERS
Bad Brad
Julie Fineman
CLIENT
L.I.F.E.—
Love Is Feeding Everyone
AGENCY/STUDIO
DMB&B LA

ART DIRECTORS
John Armistead
John Fisher
WRITER
Gary Alpern
PHOTOGRAPHER
David Leach
CLIENT
L.I.F.E.—
Love is Feeding Everyone
AGENCY/STUDIO
DMB&B LA

MAGAZINE

ART DIRECTOR
Rich Silverstein
DESIGNER
Betsy Zimmerman
WRITER
David Fowler
PHOTOGRAPHER
(Stock)
CLIENT
Royal Viking Line
AGENCY/STUDIO
Goodby, Berlin
& Silverstein

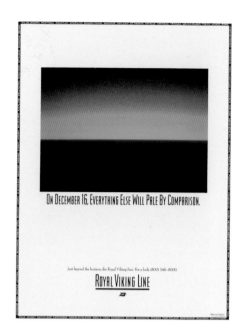

ART DIRECTOR
Betsy Zimmerman
WRITER
David Fowler
PHOTOGRAPHER
Jay Maisel
CLIENT
Royal Viking Line
AGENCY/STUDIO
Goodby, Berlin
& Silverstein

THIS DECEMBER, THE WORLD'S SHIPS WILL TAKE THEIR DIRECTION FROM A NEW SUN.

ROYAL VIKING SUN

She will be, quite simply, the most comfortable long-distance cruise liner ever built. A third larger than our present ships, she will host only four per cent more passengers. Over a third of her staterooms will have private verandas. All will have walk-in closets, television, and video cassette players. Her window-walled dining room will seat all passengers at once. There will be a private dinner club. A full spa. The only wood-burning fireplace afloat. Coming this December: the Royal Viking Sun.

For sales assistance and a copy of our handsome 1989 worldwide brochure, call (800) 346-8000. For reservations, (800) 422-8000.

ROYAL VIKING LINE

MAGAZINE

ART DIRECTOR
Steve Stone
WRITER
Jeff Goodby
PHOTOGRAPHER
(Stock)
CLIENT
Royal Viking Line
AGENCY/STUDIO
Goodby, Berlin
& Silverstein

Book 34 seats, and we'll free one up for you.

mexicana

ART DIRECTOR
Fred Burgos
WRITER
Linda Hayes
CLIENT
Mexicana Airlines
AGENCY/STUDIO
J. Walter Thompson

MAGAZINE

ART DIRECTOR
Brian Kelly

WRITER
Jim Schmidt

PHOTOGRAPHER
Gwendolyn Cates

CLIENT
Chicago Convention &
Visitors Bureau

AGENCY/STUDIO
McConnaughy
Barocci Brown

A Number Of Our Conventions Have Lost Visitors To Sharks.

It happens every year.

Driven by a desire to see all our fair city has to offer, but limited by time, large numbers of conventioneers slip away from seminars and speeches and head off seeking adventure.

Some fall prey to the sharks at the Shedd Aquarium.

Others to the lightning-quick snow leopards at the Lincoln Park Zoo.

And still others to the Museum of Natural History's giant dinosaurs.

Why, we've even heard tell of three men from Iowa who were lost to a 35-ft. boa constrictor at the Brookfield Zoo.

Obviously we have a very serious problem on our hands. But fortunately, there's a simple solution.

Conventioneers visiting Chicago should just book a few extra days onto the beginning or end of their trip.

That way, they'll be able to attend their many meetings and still have time to indulge their wanderlust.

Whether they care to walk among the shops and boutiques of Michigan Avenue, the Picassos and Rembrandts of the Art Institute, or the sunbathers and windsurfers on our many beaches.

With proper planning they may even have time to take a boat ride along our shoreline. Or to view Chicago (plus Michigan, Wisconsin and Indiana) from atop the 1454-ft. Sears Tower.

Of course, there will no doubt be those who don't heed our advice. Who don't feel they need a few extra days to see our city.

Well, to them we offer this warning: the sharks are waiting.

For more information on Chicago, and all it offers, simply call us collect at (312) 567-8500.

Or send a telex to 312-433-0306.

Chicago Convention & Visitors Bureau

ART DIRECTOR
Brian Kelly

WRITER
Jim Schmidt

PHOTOGRAPHER
Dave Jordano
Art Institute of Chicago

CLIENT
Chicago Convention &
Visitors Bureau

AGENCY/STUDIO
McConnaughy
Barocci Brown

The very same taxi ride will also take you to a Parisian Park (courtesy of Georges Seurat). A Tahitian Beach (courtesy of Paul Gauguin). And even a farm in the Midwest (courtesy of Grant Wood).

For those works of art—as well as numerous others from such folks as Picasso, Rembrandt, Toulouse-Lautrec, Degas and Van Gogh — are all part of the permanent collection at the

reach a point of museum ad nauseam, we'll simply say that you could spend a week in Chicago and still not see every dinosaur or ancient Egyptian urn we have to offer.

What about some less cultural pursuits, you ask?

Well, between our restaurants, shops, nightclubs, sports teams and lakefront you could also spend a week in our fair city and never even have

In Chicago, You Can Take A Taxi To Two Of London's Most Famous Bridges.

Art Institute of Chicago.

The Institute is just one of the many museums that make Chicago such a popular destination for convention and trade show visitors.

There's also the Field Museum of Natural History. The Museum of Contemporary Art. The Terra Museum of American Art. The Express-Ways Children's Museum. And the Museum of Science and Industry.

We could go on. But before we

time to look at a dinosaur or ancient Egyptian urn.

For more information on the many pleasures and entertainments we have to offer our convention and trade show visitors (as well as all the fine facilities we have to offer conventions and trade shows), simply call us collect at (312) 567-8500. Or telex us at 312-433-0306.

Our taxis will be standing by.

Chicago Convention & Visitors Bureau

ART DIRECTOR
Brian Kelly

WRITER
Jim Schmidt

PHOTOGRAPHER
Dave Jordano

CLIENT
Chicago Convention &
Visitors Bureau

AGENCY/STUDIO
McConnaughy
Barocci Brown

Some Of Our Most Enduring Attractions Disappear In Minutes.

In the case of the full-bodied beer seen above, it's often only a matter of seconds.

But whether it's seconds or minutes, our point is simply this: when meeting in Chicago, be prepared for culinary temptation of the highest order.

Here, for example, one can literally take one's stomach on an epicurean tour of the world.

With stops in such exotic locations as Brazil, Ethiopia, Morocco. And Thailand.

Here, one can enjoy the delicate nuances of nouvelle cuisine one evening and the not-so-subtle pleasures of

a spicy meatball sandwich the next.

Here, one can dine under the stars (at any number of outdoor cafes), under the covers (courtesy of room service at any of our first-class hotels) and under the lights (at either of our major league ball parks).

Here, in short, one can satisfy one's appetite in just about any way imaginable.

For more information on Chicago, just call us collect at (312) 567-8500. Or telex us at 433-0306.

Temptation, on a grand scale, awaits.

Chicago Convention & Visitors Bureau

In Korea, it is felt that something done with elegance, beauty and grace should also be done without interruption. So only Korean Air is offering nonstop flights every day to Seoul, Korea, from New York, Los Angeles and Honolulu. **KOREAN AIR** THE ART OF JOYFUL FLYING™

MAGAZINE

ART DIRECTORS
Tom Cordner
John Wagner

WRITER
Bill Day

ILLUSTRATOR
Tom Roberts

CLIENT
Korean Air

AGENCY/STUDIO
Ogilvy & Mather

People say we're fanatical about our beaches here in Virginia.

We do confess to some rituals that might seem excessive to others.

For example, men and women do patrol our shores here every morning. These private citizens clear away any debris left behind by man or tide. They've even been known to bring out rakes when sand needs caring for.

Virginia's beaches are swept by more than just the wind.

Of course, the people of Virginia are just as devoted to the land beyond the shoreline.

We keep the streets of nearby Colonial Williamsburg and the lawns at Monticello immaculate. We don't want anything on the Skyline Drive to distract you from the beauty of the Blue Ridge Mountains that surround you.

We keep the flame burning around the clock at Arlington National Cemetery. And we see to it that the vigil never ends at the Iwo Jima Memorial in Northern Virginia.

Naturally, you don't vacation in Virginia simply because it's clean or well-cared for. You come because the beaches are warm and close by and very inviting.

You come because your family wants to play in our giant theme parks, Busch Gardens and Kings Dominion. You come for the sheer fun of Old Town Alexandria and the Roanoke Farmers' Market. You come, perhaps, because you want your children to see Mount Vernon and Appomattox and the White House of the Confederacy. To see Jefferson's great buildings and America's great battlefields.

You come, finally, because in Virginia there are things that are fun and things that are meaningful for each and every member of your family. It's only when you leave Virginia that you find yourself talking about how nice it all was. How friendly. How clean.

For more information, call or write the Virginia Division of Tourism, Dept. J331, Richmond, VA 23219. **Virginia is for lovers ♥**

ART DIRECTOR
Jerry Torchia

PRODUCER
Vivek Rao

WRITER
Mike Hughes

PHOTOGRAPHER
Scott Barrow

CLIENT
Virginia Division
of Tourism

AGENCY/STUDIO
The Martin Agency

PRODUCTION COMPANY
Noral Color Corp.

This is an advertisement for a resort that's bigger than some states.

It's a place where backpacks and tuxedos are equally welcomed. A place where presidents, from George Washington on, have come to work and to play.

Like all good resorts, this one has swimming pools, tennis courts and world-famous golf courses.

There are, of course, quaint foot-trails here. But there's also the Skyline Drive and the Blue Ridge Parkway. Natural Bridge is here. And Daniel Boone's Wilderness Trail.

Other resorts would be proud to have five stars. This one has millions,

Air-conditioned rooms are available this summer in the Blue Ridge Mountains of Virginia.

all crystal clear in the cool night air.

No corporation owns and operates this resort: it's yours the minute you climb its mountains, walk its valleys or explore its caverns.

We're referring, of course, to the Blue Ridge Mountains and Shenandoah Valley of Virginia, a natural resort that stretches more than 200 miles through some of the most beautiful and historic land in America.

The inhabitants include more than 200 kinds of birds, more than 40 kinds of mammals, and some of the friendliest people on earth. People who speak a language that's basically English, but distinctly their own.

This year, when you consider vacations, consider this. At our unique resort, you'll picnic by gentle waterfalls and breathe in fresh mountain air. You'll be charmed by the hill country hospitality of Charlottesville and Lexington. You'll be captivated by the genius of Jefferson at Monticello and the University of Virginia. But you can't do all of this unless you come here.

to the mountains and valleys of Virginia. Where your room is already waiting for you.

For all the facts about Virginia, including information about Mount Vernon, Virginia Beach and Colonial Williamsburg, call or write the Virginia Division of Tourism, Dept. K501, Richmond, VA 23219. **Virginia is for lovers ♥**

ART DIRECTOR
Jerry Torchia

PRODUCER
Vivek Rao

WRITER
Mike Hughes

PHOTOGRAPHER
Scott Barrow

CLIENT
Virginia Division
of Tourism

AGENCY/STUDIO
The Martin Agency

PRODUCTION COMPANY
Noral Color Corp.

MAGAZINE

ART DIRECTOR
Steve Beaumont

WRITER
David Lubars

PHOTOGRAPHER
Doug Taub

CLIENT
Nissan Motor Corp.

AGENCY/STUDIO
Chiat/Day

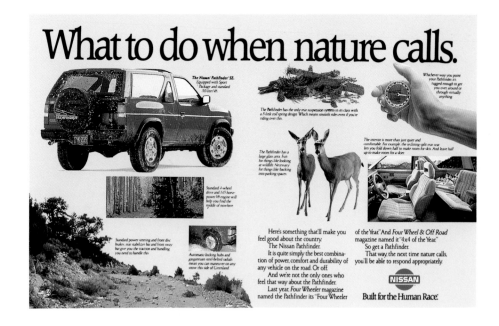

ART DIRECTOR
Steve Beaumont

WRITER
Dave Lubars

PHOTOGRAPHER
Doug Taub

CLIENT
Nissan Motor Corp.

AGENCY/STUDIO
Chiat/Day

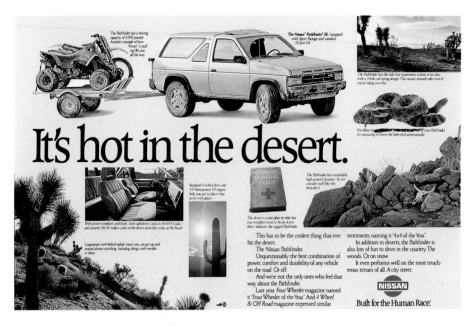

ART DIRECTOR
Pam Cunningham

WRITERS
Steve Bassett
Steve Silver

PHOTOGRAPHER
Bill Werts

CLIENT
Nissan Motor Corp.

AGENCY/STUDIO
Chiat/Day

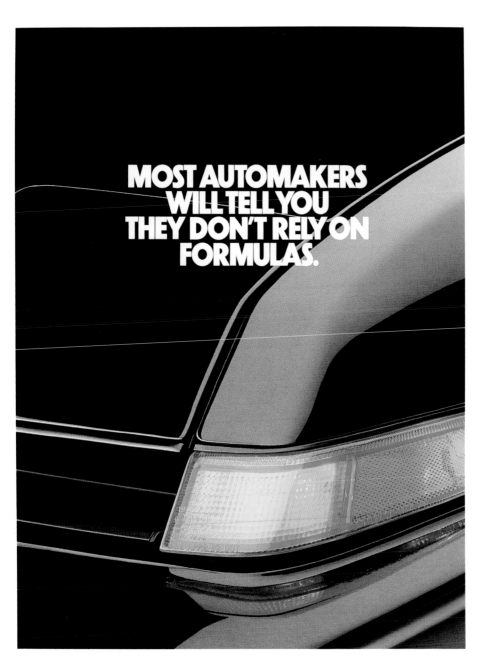

MOST AUTOMAKERS WILL TELL YOU THEY DON'T RELY ON FORMULAS.

MAYBE THAT'S BECAUSE THEY JUST HAVEN'T FOUND THE RIGHT ONE.

Building an exhilarating sports sedan is no simple task. Especially when it's one that must live up to the Acura name.

It has to look right. Feel right. Above all, it has to perform. With precision. With guts. With unprecedented excitement.

Exactly why we left our drawing boards to meet the rigorous challenges of the Formula One Grand Prix circuit.

To develop engines capable not just of beating the world's best, but dominating them, with 25 Grand Prix wins in the last three years alone.

To acquire the knowledge, the experience, and the technology essential to the development of automobiles like the Acura Integra.

With 1.6 liters, 4-valves-per-cylinder, double overhead cams, and computer-programmed fuel injection, the Integra is nothing if not race-bred.

While independent front struts, front torsion bars, front and rear stabilizer bars and equal length half shafts give you a consistent, sure-footed handle on all of that lively performance.

In fact, the Integra's combination of performance and agility can make even the most routine drive as much fun as a day at the races.

But as a quick glance in the lower right corner of this ad will tell you, the right formula doesn't stop under the hood. Consider the flush glass. Sloping hoodline. Retractable headlights. All these features contribute to the Integra's sleek good looks. And characterize its excellent aerodynamics. Its razor-sharp relationship with the wind.

Its smooth, firm, quiet ride.

Actually, this kind of functional beauty has become a major part of the Acura philosophy. A philosophy especially well realized in the Integra's interior. Intelligent ergonomics reduce driver stress. Gauges are in the natural line of vision. Controls are within easy reach. These are the results of designing a driving environment entirely around the driver.

Combine all of the above with ample leg room, plenty of space for passengers, and seats specially bolstered to keep you firmly in your place, and you're sure to find yourself cruising at a high level of comfort.

Just one more basic element of the Integra equation. In a sports sedan that owes its spirit to a not-so-basic formula.

Call 1-800-TO-ACURA for the dealer location nearest you.

ACURA
PRECISION CRAFTED PERFORMANCE
A division of American Honda Motor Co., Inc.

MAGAZINE

ART DIRECTOR
Doug Patterson

WRITER
Gail Anne Smith

PHOTOGRAPHER
Bo Hylen

CLIENT
American Honda Motor
Co., Acura Division

AGENCY/STUDIO
Ketchum Advertising

WHEN WOLFSBURG DECIDED
TO STRETCH THE LIMITATIONS OF THEIR FASTEST HATCHBACK,
THEY ASKED PIRELLI ALONG FOR THE RIDE.

Original equipment on the world's finest.

MAGAZINE

ART DIRECTOR
Michael Arola
DESIGNER
Michael Arola
WRITER
Kip Klappenback
PHOTOGRAPHER
Sean Thonson
CLIENT
Pirelli Tire Corp.
AGENCY/STUDIO
AC&R / CCL
PRODUCTION COMPANY
Jordan & Horn

For those of you who think Maseratis are just low-slung, high-priced sports cars made only for a handful of racing fanatics, we have some refreshing news.

You're only partially right.

Yes, it's true Maseratis are crafted for only a handful of people who are fanatical about owning special cars.

And, yes, they can be very quick and impressive automobiles.

But, no, the Maserati is not outrageously priced, and it's not the temperamental race car you think it is.

In fact, Maserati is a comparably priced, perfectly sane alternative to the Mercedes, Jaguar or BMW.

So while the Maserati has a well-deserved, larger-than-life image, it's a car for the real world, a car you can actually own.

The main reason there aren't many on the road, of course, is that there couldn't be. Italian craftsmen painstakingly assemble each car, doing much of the work by hand. Every part of every car is made slowly.

Except, of course, the engine. Which is made fast.

How fast? Well, the muscle under the hood of the 1989 Maserati 228 pictured here is capable of rocketing its driver to 60 mph in 6.3 seconds on its way to a top speed of 140 mph.

The 2.8 litre, electronically fuel-injected, twin-turbocharged V-6 engine can actually deliver 225 horsepower at 5500 rpm.

But this power is never reckless: it's guided by power-assisted rack and pinion steering. And the power-assisted four-wheel disc brakes hold everything in check.

What's under the hood is, however, no more remarkable than what you find behind the door of the new 228.

Inside every Maserati are seats covered with Italian glove leather that's hand-sewn by old world craftsmen, not machine-sewn by robots.

The paneling, the gearshift lever and even the parking brake handle are burled walnut or burnished rosewood.

And on the dashboard of every Maserati, just above the controls for the automatic climate control system, is a Swiss-made, jewelled clock to help you appreciate every second you spend in these plush surroundings.

While we're on the subject of time, we'd like to point out that every 1989 Maserati owner in America is now protected 24 hours a day, 365 days a year.

They're protected both by our roadside assistance program and by our 3-year/36,000 mile Maserati buyer protection plan.*

These are, of course, merely the logical reasons for owning one of our exhilarating automobiles.

The best reason might be the little voice inside your head that's been beckoning you to a Maserati ever since you were a kid.

See your dealer. And do it soon. After all, only an exclusive group will be able to buy Maseratis this year.

And, as we said, they're going fast.

There are two reasons you don't pass many Maseratis on the road. There aren't many on the road. And they are, after all, Maseratis.

You only live once. Do it in a Maserati.

ART DIRECTOR
Wayne Gibson
PRODUCER
Meredith Ott
WRITER
Luke Sullivan
PHOTOGRAPHER
Brad Miller
CLIENT
Maserati Automobile
AGENCY/STUDIO
The Martin Agency
PRODUCTION COMPANY
Graphic Process, Inc.

MAGAZINE

ART DIRECTOR
Preuit Holland

DESIGNER
Preuit Holland

WRITER
Marc Deshenes

PHOTOGRAPHER
Gary McGuire

CLIENT
Noritsu America Corp.

AGENCY/STUDIO
(213) 827-9605 &
Associates

ART DIRECTORS
Glenn Sagon
Tim Wild

DESIGNER
Glenn Sagon

WRITER
Tim Wild

PHOTOGRAPHER
Jon Exley

CLIENT
Wild Studios

AGENCY/STUDIO
EIDOLON
Advertising Inc.

DON'T BE A PEABRAIN. GET A NORITSU ENLARGER.

If you had a little 611 or 613 enlarger, you could make great big 12x18-inch prints. And whopping profits.

How whopping? How about $12 on a single enlargement?

A 12x18 in 6 minutes.

The 613 uses RA-4 chemistry, produces 187 8x10's in one hour and gives you a dry print in less than 6 minutes.

Our 611 uses standard EP-2 chemistry, turns out 71 8x10's an hour and gives you a dry print in less than 15 minutes.

Both have a spot sensor. A computer with 3,169 programmable channel combinations. And they make 1½-inch test prints. So getting a terrific enlargement the first time is real easy.

Zoom. Zoom.

Our enlarging systems also have two built-in zoom lenses and a bright viewing screen. So custom cropping is a snap, too.

And just in case you want to get into the portrait business, we even have an option that lets you do 4 wallet-size prints and 2 5x7's in a single exposure. Add an 8x10 and you've got a complete portrait package.

Support?

Naturally, like every other piece of Noritsu equipment, the 611 and 613 come with the best support in the photofinishing business.

For more information, send in the coupon. Or call (714) 521-9040.

Call somebody else and you should have your head examined.

I'm no peabrain. Tell me more about the 611 and 613 enlargers.

Name_____
Company_____
Address_____
City_____
State_____ Zip____
Phone(___)_____

THE 600 SERIES BY NORITSU
Noritsu America Corp., 6900 Noritsu Ave., Buena Park, CA 90620

IS YOUR RETOUCHER ALL THUMBS?

NEXT TIME CALL WILD STUDIOS 213-463-8109

MAGAZINE

ART DIRECTOR
Kathryn Windley

WRITER
Laurie Brandalise

PHOTOGRAPHER
Michael Ruppert

CLIENT
Microsoft

AGENCY/STUDIO
Ogilvy & Mather

If you want our help with your next presentation, we have only one thing to say.

Do it yourself.

There's a widely held theory in the business world that the key to success is knowing how to delegate.

But for the best results, there's one task we suggest you assign strictly to yourself.

Putting together your own presentations.

The easiest, most cost-efficient way to assemble a professional-looking presentation—whether it's an informal briefing or a formal new-business pitch—is to control the whole project yourself. From conception to completion, right from your own desktop.

And you won't need any help from type houses, illustrators, art departments, or typing pools.

In fact, all you'll really need is Microsoft® PowerPoint™ software and an Apple® Macintosh™ to run it.

PowerPoint gives you the power to create your own picture-perfect overhead transparencies, flip charts, 35mm color slides, speaker notes, and audience handouts. In such record-breaking time that there'll be nothing for you to do the night before the big day but sleep.

Its built-in word processor (complete with spelling checker) and drawing tools allow you to mix text and graphics in countless ways. Using different typefaces, logos, special effects like borders and dropshadows, and diagrams. Or you can copy charts, tables,

and illustrations from other programs, like Microsoft Excel, with a simple cut and paste.

You can even input entire files from Macintosh programs such as MORE™ and ThinkTank,™ and turn them directly into PowerPoint slides.

Once you design an overall "look" for your presentation, PowerPoint allows you to standardize that format automatically. So you can use it slide after slide.

And you can make global changes easily with the Slide Master, which instantly executes your revisions throughout.

At any point along the way, the Slide Sorter feature lets you view slides one by one or scan your entire presentation at a glance, or simply rearrange the order with a point and click.

Then whenever you're ready, you can print out all your presentation materials—from attention-getting overheads to handy speaker notes—without ever leaving your desk.

If 35mm slides are in order, simply send your presentation to the nearest Genigraphics® center, the leading presentation graphics service bureau, and your slides will be on their way in 48 hours.

Lastly, last-minute changes need no longer cause traditional last-minute panic. Because a PowerPoint presentation is as easy to change as it is to create.

If you'd like a live PowerPoint demonstration, call (800) 541-1261, Dept. G36, for the location of your nearest Microsoft dealer.

And remember, the best part of doing a presentation all by yourself comes afterward. When you get all the credit.

Microsoft®

Macintosh
connects.

Macintosh
connects
with personal
computers.

Macintosh
connects with
Macintosh.

Macintosh connects with Digital.

Macintosh connects with not-so-personal computers.

Best of all, Macintosh connects with you.

The most formidable challenge MIS departments face today is a difficult one, indeed:

How to bring the benefits of computers that can talk to each other to people who can't understand what they're saying.

Fortunately, a solution is at hand: Macintosh® personal computers.

Macintosh, of course, is already conversant with the human race. People love (yes, "love," a term you won't find in the MS-DOS glossary) its graphic, intuitive and consistent way of working.

Their employers, in turn, appreciate how that affection translates into training and support costs as much as 25% lower than MS-DOS PCs.

But now this Macintosh advantage extends far beyond the desktop. To networks of every shape, size and configuration. Not to mention computers of every brand name.

THE NETWORK THAT WORKS BETTER FOR WORKGROUPS.

Everybody knows that people get more accomplished when they work together.

Why should computers be any different?

So Apple Workgroup Computing unites them with some qualities that you used to find only in people: cooperation and flexibility.

Team spirit, captured in the AppleTalk® Network System and the AppleShare® File Server.

AppleTalk conforms to the OSI reference model and it can link your workgroup together in whatever way works best for you: twisted-pair, fiber optics, Ethernet, you name it.

AppleShare is the very definition of transparency. Allowing Macintosh users to exchange information and access network resources in the point-and-click manner Macintosh made famous.

So people spend their time utilizing the network, instead of learning it.

Add AppleShare PC software to your MS-DOS PCs and they fit right in. Because AppleShare lets Macintosh and MS-DOS PCs swap information almost as easily as Macintosh and Macintosh.

With AppleShare, everyone works in the environment they know best. MS-DOS directories appear on a Macintosh screen as file folders. Macintosh folders, in turn, appear on an MS-DOS screen as directories.

So your local area network isn't just local. It's neighborly.

But not too neighborly. Because Apple-Share has powerful access controls. To let the owner of a file decide who, if anyone, may read it or change it.

THE DEC CONNECTION.

The recent alliance between Apple® and Digital Equipment Corporation simply formalized something most of the world already knew: Macintosh is one of the most elegant ways to tap the power of VAX® and other minicomputers.

A Digital VAX can operate as an AppleShare-compatible file server. Or, Macintosh can be connected directly to DECnet.® You can use Macintosh as a front-end to Digital's All-In-One Office Automation System. Or use Apple's revolutionary HyperCard® software to customize a Macintosh front-end to a VAX SQL database.

The list goes on. But whatever option MIS chooses to meet their specific needs, it all looks the same. That is, just like a Macintosh.

A TRANSPARENT ATTEMPT TO WIN YOU OVER.

On a Macintosh screen, mainframe resources appear no more intimidating than a floppy disk. And they're just as easy to work with.

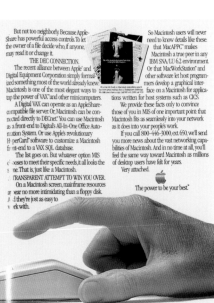

So Macintosh users will never need to know details like these: that MacAPPC makes Macintosh a true peer in any IBM SNA/LU 6.2 environment. Or that MacWorkStation® and other software let host programmers develop a graphical interface on a Macintosh for applications written for host systems such as CICS.

We provide these facts only to convince those of you in MIS of one important point: that Macintosh fits as seamlessly into your network as it does into your people's work.

If you call 800-446-3000, ext. 650, we'll send you more news about the vast networking capabilities of Macintosh. And in no time at all, you'll feel the same way toward Macintosh as millions of desktop users have felt for years.

Very attached.

The power to be your best.™

MAGAZINE
DESIGNER
Ivan Horvath
PRODUCER
Karen Garnett
WRITER
Ken Segall
PHOTOGRAPHER
Gary McGuire
CLIENT
Apple Computer Inc.
AGENCY/STUDIO
BBDO LA

ART DIRECTOR
Kathy Aird
PRODUCER
Karen Garnett
WRITER
Laurie Brandalise
PHOTOGRAPHER
Terry Heffernan
CLIENT
Apple Computer Inc.
AGENCY/STUDIO
BBDO LA

In 1988 you can change the course of History.

MAGAZINE
ART DIRECTOR
Jon Reeder
PRODUCER
Karen Garnett
WRITERS
Robert Chandler
Rob Siltanen
PHOTOGRAPHER
Paul Taylor
CLIENT
Apple Computer Inc.
AGENCY/STUDIO
BBDO LA

Or anything else you're teaching.

When papyrus replaced clay tablets, there was no end of excitement in the faculty lounges of Sumer.

Here was a development that lightened the work load, made homework less burdensome, and just generally made teaching less of a grind.

Well, now that Mankind has had another 5000 years to mull over the problems of educators, there has appeared another development of perhaps equal significance. Curriculum software or "courseware" that runs on the Macintosh personal computer.

Created by academics teaching in many diverse disciplines and subjects, courseware transcends the limitations of paper. Because courseware exists on a dynamic medium, it can do things that traditional textbooks can't.

The complete course in courseware.

If this ad were on a courseware disk instead of on paper, it could respond to almost any questions you might have on the subject of courseware itself.

It could simulate courseware programs showing you exactly how they work. It could even teach you, step by step, to write courseware for yourself.

Courseware stimulates excitement, intensity, and greater involvement in the process of learning. The more complex the subject you're teaching, the more courseware can help you in teaching it.

All this from a pocket-sized disk that costs about the same price as an ordinary textbook.

There are two ways you can start bringing these benefits into your classroom now.

The first way is through Kinko's Academic Courseware Exchange. In the *Courseware Exchange Catalog* you'll find an extensive electronic library, created by your colleagues, offering over 150 titles in a broad range of subjects. From building a bridge to breaking down a molecule to staging a play.

The second way is by writing your own courseware. A project which no longer requires any programming experience thanks to a new generation of software authoring tools.

These include *HyperCard,* *Course Builder, Course of Action, Guide,* and *VideoWorks Interactive.*

Combine them with your own expertise and you'll be able to create in as little as a month what used to take more than a year.

If you think you might like to try your hand at this, Apple has published the *Guide to Courseware Authoring,* which explains just what's required to get started.

Then, after we've shown you how courseware authoring has been made easier, we'll explain how it can be made more rewarding.

Just crack open the *Academic Courseware Exchange Developer's Handbook,* and read how Kinko's can help you distribute your courseware to campuses across the nation.

Which is a very good way to let everyone profit from your knowledge and experience.

Everyone. Including you. Through the royalties your work generates.

Both these books, along with the catalog, are yours free. All you've got to do is ask for them.

So feel free to call for the set at 800-732-3131, Ext. 700. And we'll send you the complete course.

We invite you to take the first step towards revolutionizing the way you teach your own classes.

Who knows, you might just earn your name a place in the history disks.

The power to be your best.™

Just A Few Of Our 24-Hour Loan Information Centers.

As you know, real estate can sometimes be a real 9 to 5 job. 9pm to 5am.

Which is exactly why California Federal loan reps are now giving out some very special numbers.

Namely, their home phone numbers. So now if something "can't wait till Monday morning" it doesn't have to. Handle it on Saturday. Or Sunday. With a simple, local phone call.

And what if nobody's home? We can always beep your California Federal loan rep on a 24-hour pager. They're that accessible. And that committed to helping you close.

So the next time you have trouble contacting your current loan rep, give California Federal a call. Because we're very proud of our new business hours.

All 24 of them.

CALIFORNIA FEDERAL
Well Managed Money.

When You Call For Loan Status You'll Get Our Answering Machine.

"Where's my client's loan?" "Is the appraisal done?" "What documents do you need?" "When do we close?" "How much longer?"

Good questions.

California Federal's answer? A computerized loan status network with thousands of miles of computer cable linking hundreds of terminals for one reason:

Loan status.

Up-to-the-second loan status. Call your California Federal loan center with a question and within seconds we'll be in front of a terminal punching out an answer.

So we can give you the who, what, when, where, why and how. Now.

We'll also give you the convenience of reaching your loan rep on a 24-hour pager.

It's all part of our total commitment to helping you sell more homes. More quickly. More smoothly. More frequently.

For more information, just pick up the phone and call California Federal. And don't worry.

You won't get an answering machine.

CALIFORNIA FEDERAL
Well Managed Money.

To Make Our Loan Reps Easy To Find, They All Wear The Same Thing.

California Federal just made your job a whole lot easier. By making our loan reps a whole lot easier to reach.

With 24-hour pagers.

Now if your questions just can't wait, they don't have to. Just pick up the phone and get ahold of a loan rep and an answer. Anytime. Anyplace. Weeknights or weekends.

At California Federal, we've never been more committed to helping you close your deals.

We've added a computer system to track loan status much quicker, and more accurately.

We're also offering a wide selection of loans, so we can tailor our services to your client, instead of the other way around.

And, every single one of our loan reps is on commission. So they're just as motivated, dedicated and committed as you are.

So take a look at our loan reps and what they have on. After all, a great deal shouldn't be lost because your loan rep can't be found.

CALIFORNIA FEDERAL
Well Managed Money.

MAGAZINE
CAMPAIGN

ART DIRECTOR
Jerry Torchia
PRODUCER
Vivek Rao
WRITER
Mike Huges
PHOTOGRAPHER
Scott Barrow
CLIENT
Virginia Division of
Tourism
AGENCY/STUDIO
The Martin Agency
PRODUCTION COMPANY
Noral Color Corp.

This is an advertisement for a resort that's bigger than some states.

It's a place where backpacks and tuxedos are equally welcomed. A place where presidents, from George Washington on, have come to work and to play.

Like all good resorts, this one has swimming pools, tennis courts and world-famous golf courses.

There are, of course, quaint foot-trails here. But there's also the Skyline Drive and the Blue Ridge Parkway. Natural Bridge is here. And Daniel Boone's Wilderness Trail.

Other resorts would be proud to have five stars. This one has millions,

Air-conditioned rooms are available this summer in the Blue Ridge Mountains of Virginia.

all crystal clear in the cool night air.

No corporation owns and operates this resort: it's yours the minute you climb its mountains, walk its valleys or explore its caverns.

We're referring, of course, to the Blue Ridge Mountains and Shenandoah Valley of Virginia, a natural resort that stretches more than 200 miles through some of the most beautiful and historic land in America.

The inhabitants include more than 200 kinds of birds, more than 40 kinds of mammals, and some of the friendliest people on earth. People who speak a language that's basically English, but distinctly their own.

This year, when you consider vacations, consider this. At our unique resort, you'll picnic by gentle waterfalls and breathe in fresh mountain air. You'll be charmed by the hill country hospitality of Charlottesville and Lexington. You'll be captivated by the genius of Jefferson at Monticello and the University of Virginia. But you can't do all of this unless you come here, to the mountains and valleys of Virginia. Where your room is already waiting for you.

For all the facts about Virginia, including information about Mount Vernon, Virginia Beach and Colonial Williamsburg, call or write the Virginia Division of Tourism, Dept. R501, Richmond, VA 23219.

Virginia is for lovers ♥

Listen to the names. Jamestown. Colonial Williamsburg. The American Revolution. Yorktown. Mount Vernon. Monticello. The Civil War. Richmond. The White House of the Confederacy. Manassas. Appomattox.

You've been playing with the idea of a Virginia vacation for a long, long time.

Once upon a time, when you were just beginning to understand what America was all about, these were the names that introduced you to her past.

Gradually, you connected these places and events to other names. George Washington and Thomas Jefferson. Patrick Henry and James Madison. Robert E. Lee. Stonewall Jackson and Jefferson Davis.

On a vacation in Virginia, you'll find yourself playing with the past all over again. The soldiers and the presidents and the rebels will once again come alive in your mind and in your heart.

You'll board the Susan Constant at Jamestown. You'll walk the elegant halls of the Governor's Palace in Williamsburg. You'll explore the historic battlefields of Petersburg and the elegant plantation homes of some of the men and women who built America.

Of course, since you'll be doing all of this in Virginia, there will always be other pleasant surprises just around the corner.

You'll enjoy our beaches and our Blue Ridge Mountains. The Barter Theatre and The Waterside Festival Marketplace. Our theme parks, Busch Gardens and Kings Dominion. There is a part of you that's been waiting for a vacation like this for a long, long time.

Come to Virginia now and return to the past. America's past—and your own.

For more information about Virginia's historic attractions, mountains, beaches and world-class resorts, just call or write the Virginia Division of Tourism, Dept. L511, Richmond, VA 23219.

Virginia is for lovers ♥

People say we're fanatical about our beaches here in Virginia.

We do confess to some rituals that might seem excessive to others.

For example, men and women do patrol our shores here every morning. These private citizens clear away any debris left behind by man or tide. They've even been known to bring out rakes when sand needs caring for.

Virginia's beaches are swept by more than just the wind.

Of course, the people of Virginia are just as devoted to the land beyond the shoreline.

We keep the streets of nearby Colonial Williamsburg and the lawns at Monticello immaculate. We don't want anything on the Skyline Drive to distract you from the beauty of the Blue Ridge Mountains that surround you.

We keep the flame burning around the clock at Arlington National Cemetery. And we see to it that the vigil never ends at the Iwo Jima Memorial in Northern Virginia.

Naturally, you don't vacation in Virginia simply because it's clean or well-cared for. You come because the beaches are warm and close by and very inviting.

You come because your family wants to play in our giant theme parks, Busch Gardens and Kings Dominion. You come for the sheer fun of Old Town Alexandria and the Roanoke Farmer's Market. You come, perhaps, because you want your children to see Mount Vernon and Appomattox and the White House of the Confederacy. To see Jefferson's great buildings and America's great battlefields.

You come, finally, because in Virginia there are things that are fun and things that are meaningful for each and every member of your family. It's only when you leave Virginia that you find yourself talking about how nice it all was. How friendly. How clean.

For more information, call or write the Virginia Division of Tourism, Dept. J331, Richmond, VA 23219.

Virginia is for lovers ♥

ADVERTISING

MAGAZINE
CAMPAIGN

ART DIRECTORS
Gary Goldsmith
Mike Rosen

DESIGNERS
Gary Goldsmith
Mike Rosen

WRITERS
Neal Gomberg
Mike Rosen

CLIENT
Citizens Against
Cocaine Abuse

AGENCY/STUDIO
Goldsmith/Jeffrey

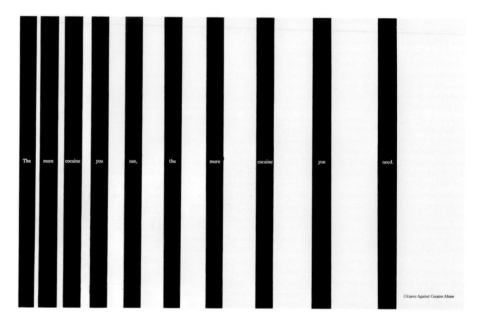

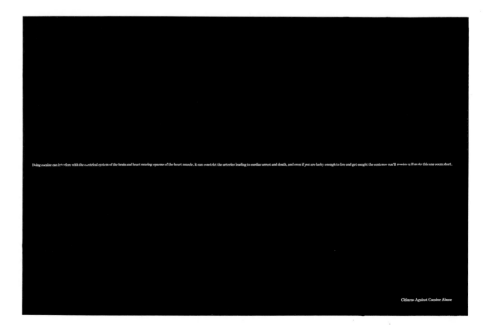

THIS IS A THREAT.

THIS IS A PROMISE.

Today our adversaries have in place a multi-layer gauntlet of surface-to-air weaponry. The most formidable that has ever existed.

They are reinforcing a two-to-one numerical advantage in fighters and interceptors with significant qualitative advances.

These include new air-to-air missiles, state-of-the-art sensors, and new look-down, shoot-down capabilities. All linked together in a vast network of C³ systems.

This is the threat the Advanced Tactical Fighter must nullify.

Flying undetected for long distances at sustained supersonic speeds, it will disrupt and destroy entire enemy formations massing for attack. The ATF will gain and maintain air superiority providing a clean corridor for friendly forces.

The USAF team of Northrop and McDonnell Douglas brings to the ATF project its ten year F/A-18 partnership. And a heritage of thousands of frontline fighters, including F-4's, F-5's, F-15's and F/A-18's.

Denying the skies to any foe is the mission of the Advanced Tactical Fighter. The Northrop/McDonnell **NORTHROP** Douglas ATF will accomplish that mission. *The Northrop/McDonnell Douglas ATF Team*

WE CAN'T SHOW YOU WHAT WE'RE DOING,

BUT WE CAN SHOW YOU WHAT WE'VE DONE.

We cannot display it, or diagram it, or illustrate it.

Nor are we publishing any photographs. And even when it flies, it will be virtually undetectable.

The Advanced Tactical Fighter.

F-23 prototypes being built for the Air Force by Northrop and McDonnell Douglas represent our forty years of experience building combat aircraft.

And, in fact, we have more fighter experience between us than any other

manufacturers in the free world today.

A heritage of thousands of frontline fighters. Including the F-4, the F-5, the F-15. And the F/A-18, the product of our ten year partnership. When deployed, the F-23 will deliver the decisive

edge. Where the enemy has both superior numbers and technological parity, it is the edge that will be essential if we are to prevail.

ATF-23
The Northrop/McDonnell Douglas Team

HOW TO FLY THE UNFRIENDLY SKIES.

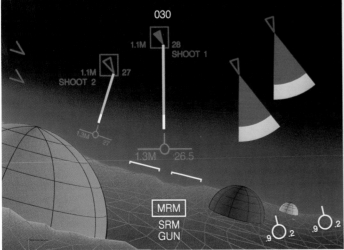

In future air warfare, cockpit systems will be capable of interpreting large quantities of information, presented on multi-function displays, that can be both understood and responded to instantly.

The Advanced Tactical Fighter will enhance the pilot's awareness in combat. Allowing him to prioritize targets, to recognize threats, and to avoid areas of greatest peril.

The ATF's supercruise performance and low observability will enable our pilots to see the enemy first. And to shoot first.

Squadrons of threat aircraft will be neutralized when they are massing for attack. Then, under the air superiority umbrella provided by ATFs, our existing air and ground forces can effectively accomplish their missions.

YF-23A prototypes are now being built for the U.S. Air Force by the team of Northrop and McDonnell Douglas.

Agile, swift, and hard to detect, the Advanced Tactical Fighter will rewrite the terms of tomorrow's air warfare.

On our terms.

NORTHROP YF-23A
The Northrop/McDonnell Douglas ATF Team

MAGAZINE CAMPAIGN

ART DIRECTOR
Yvonne Smith
PRODUCER
Karen Garnett
WRITER
Robert Chandler
PHOTOGRAPHER
Jim Hall
Lamb & Hall
CLIENT
Northrop Corp.
AGENCY/STUDIO
BBDO LA

ART DIRECTOR
Yvonne Smith
PRODUCER
Karen Garnett
WRITER
Robert Chandler
CLIENT
Northrop Corp.
AGENCY/STUDIO
BBDO LA

ART DIRECTOR
Yvonne Smith
PRODUCER
Karen Garnett
WRITER
Robert Chandler
PHOTOGRAPHER
Jim Hall
ILLUSTRATOR
Chris Davey
CLIENT
Northrop Corp.
AGENCY/STUDIO
BBDO LA

What to do when nature calls.

Here's something that'll make you feel good about the country.
The Nissan Pathfinder.
It is quite simply the best combination of power, comfort and durability of any vehicle on the road. Or off.
And we're not the only ones who feel that way about the Pathfinder.
Last year, *Four Wheeler* magazine named the Pathfinder its "Four Wheeler of the Year." And *Four Wheel & Off Road* magazine named it "4x4 of the Year."
So get a Pathfinder.
That way, the next time nature calls, you'll be able to respond appropriately.

NISSAN
Built for the Human Race.

It's hot in the desert.

This has to be the coolest thing that ever hit the desert.
The Nissan Pathfinder.
Unquestionably the best combination of power, comfort and durability of any vehicle on the road. Or off.
And we're not the only ones who feel that way about the Pathfinder.
Last year, *Four Wheeler* magazine named it "Four Wheeler of the Year." And *4 Wheel & Off Road* magazine expressed similar sentiments, naming it "4x4 of the Year."
In addition to deserts, the Pathfinder is also lots of fun to drive in the country. The woods. Or on snow.
It even performs well on the most treacherous terrain of all. A city street.

NISSAN
Built for the Human Race.

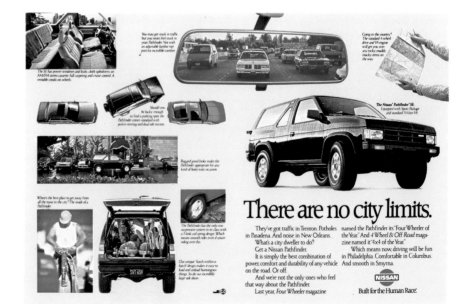

There are no city limits.

They've got traffic in Trenton. Potholes in Pasadena. And noise in New Orleans.
What's a city dweller to do?
Get a Nissan Pathfinder.
It is simply the best combination of power, comfort and durability of any vehicle on the road. Or off.
And we're not the only ones who feel that way about the Pathfinder.
Last year, *Four Wheeler* magazine named the Pathfinder its "Four Wheeler of the Year." And *4 Wheel & Off Road* magazine named it "4x4 of the Year."
Which means now, driving will be fun in Philadelphia. Comfortable in Columbus. And smooth in Smyrna.

NISSAN
Built for the Human Race.

Oil crisis averted by Macintosh.

These days, in spite of the dizzying gyrations of OPEC, the U.S. oil industry has managed to strike gold at home. With Macintosh® personal computers.

Resourceful companies such as ARCO are finding that Macintosh really can help with most everything.

From determining drilling sites and designing refinery equipment to handling routine office tasks like spreadsheets and desktop publishing.

Like other *Fortune 500* companies, they're even finding that Macintosh maximizes prior computer investments. Because it can communicate with MS-DOS computers and mainframes.

Macintosh also has a lower training cost per desktop than any MS-DOS computer—prompting some spectacular jumps in productivity. In a recent in-depth analysis of selected Macintosh installations in business, users consistently reported productivity increases of 15%-25% and more.

Now that you know why oil and Macintosh mix so well, call 800-446-3000, ext. 400, for an authorized Apple reseller. And avoid a crisis of your own.

The power to be your best.™

Macintosh used as food processor.

It's quickly becoming the hottest desk appliance in the U.S. food industry.

Because it can do literally hundreds of jobs. Everything from designing packages to ordering sugar and spice by the ton.

In fact, companies like the Sara Lee Corporation and Pillsbury have put in dozens of Macintosh® personal computers.

They've found that Macintosh's incredible appetite for work is satisfied by all the latest business software.

And that it can unify a sprawling enterprise with its very own low cost network. Or by communicating with MS-DOS computers and mainframes.

Macintosh also has a lower training cost per desktop than any MS-DOS computer—prompting some spectacular jumps in productivity. In an in-depth analysis of selected Macintosh installations in business, users consistently reported productivity increases of 15%-25% and more. Food for thought for any business.

Why not call 800-446-3000 ext. 400 for the nearest authorized Apple® reseller.

And finish processing all the facts.

The power to be your best.™

Big Eight accountants refuse to write off Macintosh.

Some people still think there's only one way to crunch numbers: a computer with initials. But several major accounting firms like Arthur Young & Company have been adding Macintosh® personal computers by the hundreds.

Because the companies that best understand numbers, understand what Macintosh can bring to the bottom line.

Macintosh has a lower training cost per desktop than any MS-DOS computer—prompting some spectacular jumps in productivity. In a recent in-depth analysis of selected Macintosh installations in business, users consistently reported productivity increases of 15%-25% and more.

Auditors take Macintosh computers with them into the field so they can perform on-the-spot analyses. Working with text and numbers directly from clients' mainframes or MS-DOS computers.

Back at the home office, Apple® Desktop Publishing turns out documents and presentations that can make even balance sheets look exciting.

Perhaps you should call 800-446-3000. Extension 400 for an authorized Apple reseller near you. Because whatever business you're in, it pays to know what the accountants are up to.

The power to be your best.™

MAGAZINE CAMPAIGN

ART DIRECTOR
Kathy Aird

PRODUCER
Karen Garnett

WRITER
Laurie Brandalise

PHOTOGRAPHER
Terry Heffernan

CLIENT
Apple Computer Inc.

AGENCY/STUDIO
BBDO LA

Basically, we took the same idea and added carpeting.

NISSAN
Built for the Human Race.

At a time when many cars have no personality, here's one with several.

Most people who buy economy cars are missing a few screws.

NISSAN
Built for the Human Race.

Manhattan Transfer.

Rush hour in Manhattan. It *never* rushes. And it's never *ever* just an hour. Some days, a pigeon couldn't thread its way through traffic with a crowbar.

In the midst of this ordeal, there are more Mercedes-Benz trucks plying their trade than in any other city in America.

That's because Manhattan's street-smart businessmen know a good deal when they see it. Mercedes-Benz trucks are competitively priced and cost less to operate. They can cruise at full throttle or idle continually, day and night, with incredible reliability. They introduce drivers to a new trucking experience called comfort.

Mercedes-Benz trucks are assembled in America. Backed by the best warranty.* Supported by the most competent parts supply network in the business — including money-where-our-mouth-is Guaranteed Parts Availability.†

Not everyone has what it takes to make it in New York. But everyone wants a truck that does.

To transfer what we do for Manhattan to your own grueling pace, see our complete line of trucks at your Mercedes-Benz Truck Dealer today.

MERCEDES-BENZ TRUCKS

Making it big in the Big Apple.

Brooklyn Dodger.

Take Rhode Island. Double its population. Quadruple its industry. Add the busiest port in America. Then shrink it all to *one-twelfth* the size.

Welcome to Brooklyn. A nice place to visit, *if* you can steer clear of the clutter of machines and humanity that clogs the streets night and day.

Artful dodging like this is one reason Mercedes-Benz easily sells more trucks in New York than in any other city in America.

Mercedes-Benz trucks offer some of the sharpest turning angles and best visibility in their class, with power steering standard. While most trucks are patchwork assemblies of parts, all major Mercedes-Benz components are engineered to work together.

They are assembled in America. Backed by strongest warranty of their kind.* And offer Guaranteed Parts Availability§ through a nationwide truck dealer network nearly 200 strong.

In New York, prestige alone won't make it to first base. Our trucks made it on a competitive price. On proven reliability. By dodging trouble and delivering the goods.

See them for yourself at your Mercedes-Benz Truck Dealer today.

MERCEDES-BENZ TRUCKS

Making it big in the Big Apple.

The Toast of New York.

New Yorkers don't have much patience with out-of-towners. On the other hand, they admire anyone who can get around the big city without spending a fortune or wasting time.

That's why Mercedes-Benz trucks hold a higher share of market in New York than in any other city of America. They've got everything it takes to survive a sea of humanity seven million strong.

So if you thought Mercedes-Benz trucks were designed and priced for, say, transporting polo ponies in East Hampton, think again.

With their competitive price, and tightwad fuel consumption, stalwart reliability and exceptional warranty,* Mercedes-Benz makes most other trucks look more like tourist traps.

Mercedes-Benz trucks are assembled in America as integrated machines, not as patchwork collections of OEM parts. They are distinctively maneuverable. Comfortable. Backed nationwide by some 200 dealerships and Guaranteed Parts Availability.†

Put their acclaimed economy to work for you. Take a test drive soon at your Mercedes-Benz Truck Dealer.

MERCEDES-BENZ TRUCKS

Making it big in the Big Apple.

MAGAZINE
CAMPAIGN

ART DIRECTOR
Frank Roehr

CLIENT MGR.
Robert Warner

WRITER
Brian Mount

PHOTOGRAPHER
Karl Sandell

CLIENT
Mercedes-Benz Truck Co.

AGENCY/STUDIO
Young & Roehr, Inc.

*MAGAZINE
CAMPAIGN*

ART DIRECTOR
Jeff Gree & Mike Malatak

DIRECTOR
Creative Director:
Dan Heagy

WRITERS
Donna Speigel
Bob Welke

CLIENT
Procter & Gamble
Pepto-Bismol

AGENCY/STUDIO
Leo Burnett Company

The one that coats
is the only one you need.

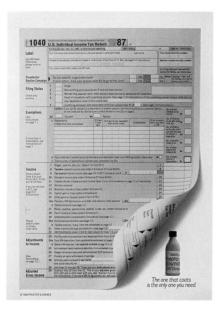

Cream good enough for Colombian Coffee isn't exactly easy to find.

Ever since she was a mere calf, she's had a problem making friends. All the other cows just assumed she wouldn't give them the time of day.

After all, they know who Juan Valdez® is. It's where they spend their entire lives wishing their cream would go. Into Colombian Coffee, that is.

And if you told any one of these cows that millions of Americans are willing to pay a premium for *the richest coffee in the world*," they probably wouldn't even blink an eye.

But enough of cows.

You want to know how much your profits could rise from keeping a man and his mule around?

Remember when the cow jumped over the moon?

For more information write to: 100% Colombian Coffee Program, P.O. Box 8545, NY, NY 10150. Or call 1-800-223-3101.

*MAGAZINE
CAMPAIGN*

ART DIRECTOR
Sharon L. Occhipinti

DESIGNER
Sharon L. Occhipinti

WRITER
Susan Leiker

PHOTOGRAPHER
Stuart Heir

CLIENT
Nat. Fed. Coffee Growers

AGENCY/STUDIO
DDBN, NY

100% Obsessed.

After fifteen minutes of clipping and snipping, he finally granted us an interview.

"It all started with my first cup of 100% Colombian Coffee. After that, I drank it any way I could. Hot. Iced. It really didn't matter to me."

We thought we should tell him he wasn't alone. That half of America is willing to pay a premium for *the richest coffee in the world*." But all he could say to that was "What's wrong with the other half?"

Guys like these.

They're the ones who make keeping 100% Colombian Coffee around 100% worthwhile.

For more information write to: 100% Colombian Coffee, P.O. Box 8545, NY, NY 10150. Or call 1-800-223-3101.

ART DIRECTOR
Sharon L. Occhipinti

DESIGNER
Sharon L. Occhipinti

WRITER
Susan Leiker

PHOTOGRAPHER
Jim Porto

CLIENT
Nat. Fed. Coffee Growers

AGENCY/STUDIO
DDBN, NY

Signs of intelligent life.

As they moved closer to what they thought to be an abnormally shaped crater, all three astronauts seemed to smile at once.

After all, it's what every astronaut has hoped to find.

Not Juan Valdez® per se, but some sign of intelligence on a planet other than earth.

Filled with excitement, they thought not of the roasters who have prospered from keeping *the richest coffee in the world*" around, but of their own fame and fortune that might come as a result.

With that in mind, toasting their success with a steaming hot cup of Colombian Coffee seemed like a very intelligent idea indeed.

For more information write to: 100% Colombian Coffee Program, P.O. Box 8545, New York, New York 10150. Or call 1-800-223-3101.

ART DIRECTOR
Sharon L. Occhipinti

DESIGNER
Sharon L. Occhipinti

WRITER
Susan Leiker

PHOTOGRAPHER
Raymond Mier
(Stock) NASA

CLIENT
Nat. Fed. Coffee Growers

AGENCY/STUDIO
DDBN, NY

OUTDOOR

ART DIRECTOR
Andy Dijak
WRITER
Bill Stenton
PHOTOGRAPHER
Jeffrey Zwart
CLIENT
Porsche Cars
North America
AGENCY/STUDIO
Chiat/Day

Porsche 911

ART DIRECTOR
Jordin Mendelsohn
WRITER
Jordin Mendelsohn
CLIENT
Penguin's Frozen Yogurt
AGENCY/STUDIO
Mendelsohn/Zien

OUTDOOR

ART DIRECTOR
Jordin Mendelsohn
WRITER
Jordin Mendelsohn
CLIENT
Southern California
Acura Dealers
AGENCY/STUDIO
Mendelsohn/Zien

ART DIRECTORS
Richard Crispo
David Toyoshima
WRITER
Bob Ancona
PHOTOGRAPHER
Bo Hylen
CLIENT
American Honda Motor
Co., Acura Division
AGENCY/STUDIO
Ketchum Advertising

ART DIRECTORS
Richard Crispo
David Toyoshima
WRITERS
Scott Aal
Bob Ancona
PHOTOGRAPHER
Bo Hylen
CLIENT
American Honda Motor
Co., Acura Division
AGENCY/STUDIO
Ketchum Advertising

DIRECT MAIL

CREATIVE DIRECTOR
Paul Pruneau

ART DIRECTOR
Rob Smiley

ACCOUNT MANAGER
Sue Rundstadler

PRODUCTION COORDINATOR
Nicki Riedel

WRITER
Rich Binell

PHOTOGRAPHER
Bruce Ashley

PRODUCTION ART
Dave Lambing

CLIENT
Apple Computer, Inc.

To capitalize on
an emerging market,
you have to be
in the right place
at the right time.

Here's the place.

We'll hold a seat just for you
at the Moscone Center
747 Howard Street
San Francisco, CA 94103

Here's the time.

We'll begin at 7:00 A.M. on May 4.
And you'll be busy till nine.
Please don't be late.

And here's the market.

This market opportunity is virtually unlimited.
But seats at the Apple CPA Briefing aren't.

So call 800-446-3000, ext. 800.

There
are some things you just can't get from books.

DIRECT MAIL

ART DIRECTOR
Devin Ivester

DESIGNER
Devin Ivester

WRITER
Rob Price

CLIENT
Apple Computer, Inc.

PRODUCTION MANAGER
JoAnn Hogue

DIRECT MAIL

ART DIRECTOR
Wayne Gibson
PRODUCER
Vivek Rao
WRITER
Luke Sullivan
PHOTOGRAPHER
Wayne Gibson
CLIENT
Dave Martin
AGENCY/STUDIO
The Martin Agency

Return To A Time
When You Had
Basketball In
The Gym, Football
On The Field

And Gymnastics Here.

ART DIRECTOR
Cris Morales
DESIGNER
Cris Morales
WRITER
Eric J. Kiker
CLIENT
Eric J. Kiker
AGENCY/STUDIO
EJK

To become
a copywriter who's
versatile, sharp and
handy in a crisis,
I've modeled myself
after an expert
in the field.

Eric James Kiker.
writer

DIRECT MAIL

ART DIRECTOR
Jennifer Morla

DESIGNER
Jennifer Morla

WRITER
Ann Ure

CLIENT
Levi Strauss & Co.

AGENCY/STUDIO
Morla Design, Inc.

POINT OF PURCHASE,
DISPLAY

ART DIRECTOR
Laura Della Sala

WRITER
Rob Feakins

PHOTOGRAPHER
Gary McGuire

CLIENT
Foster Farms Poultry

AGENCY/STUDIO
Chiat/Day

ART DIRECTOR
Laura Della Sala

WRITER
Rob Feakins

PHOTOGRAPHER
Gary McGuire

CLIENT
Foster Farms Poultry

AGENCY/STUDIO
Chiat/Day

BROCHURE, FOLDER
CREATIVE DIRECTOR
Paul Pruneau
ART DIRECTOR
Paul Pruneau
PRODUCTION
COORDINATOR
Charlie Dana
WRITER
Steve Goldstein
PRODUCTION ART
Andrea Kelly
CLIENT
Apple Computer, Inc.
AGENCY/STUDIO
Apple Creative Services

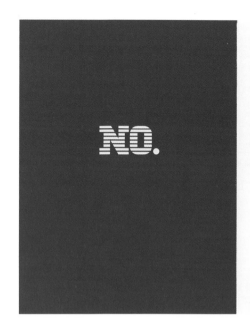

ART DIRECTOR
Carol Golden
DESIGNERS
Carol Golden
Paul Pruneau
ILLUSTRATOR
Geoffrey Moss
CLIENT
Apple Computer Co.

ART DIRECTOR
Vigon/Seireeni
DESIGNER
Vigon/Seireeni
PHOTOGRAPHER
Phillip Dixon
CLIENT
Leon Max
AGENCY/STUDIO
Vigon/Seireeni

There's a Yamaha system for every stage of your career.

Not too long ago, playing music was about as simple as picking up an instrument and walking on stage. Then two things happened.

Electricity. And MIDI.

True, things have become a little more complicated as a result.

But most musicians would be quick to agree that the creative climate has never been better.

In fact, thanks to MIDI, you can write and perform in ways the masters never dreamed.

You can edit your music with absolute control over every note, every nuance. Gain the freedom to experiment with new and different sounds. Even go so far as to redefine what is physically possible for your fingers to play.

There's only one catch. To take advantage of what MIDI can do, you need more than an instrument.

You need a system.

And that's what this whole catalog is all about. It's filled with Yamaha digital systems for every point in your musical career.

From your first composition to your first world tour.

It's a catalog that only Yamaha could produce. The reason being, only Yamaha offers a complete line of MIDI products designed to work together.

Not just synthesizers and electronic pianos. But sequencers, digital drum machines, tape decks, mixers, sound processing equipment and every last accessory.

So whatever your experience, take a good look at the pages that follow. You're sure to find everything you need to tap the power of MIDI.

And make the move up to the next stage.

BROCHURE, FOLDER

ART DIRECTOR
Ivan Horvath

PRODUCER
Karen Garnett

WRITER
Ken Segall

PHOTOGRAPHERS
Gary McGuire
David Leach
Jay Silverman

CLIENT
Yamaha Digital
Musical Instruments

AGENCY/STUDIO
BBDO LA

DESIGNER
Rich Nelson

WRITER
Rob Price

PHOTOGRAPHER
Bruce Ashley

CLIENT
Apple Computer, Inc.

PRODUCTION MANAGER
Barbara Crow

POSTER

ART DIRECTOR
Carol Mack

WRITER
Melanie Marnich

CLIENT
Minikahda Storage

AGENCY/STUDIO
Carol Mack Advertising

ART DIRECTOR
Michael Arola

DESIGNER
Michael Arola

WRITER
Kip Klappenback

ILLUSTRATOR
Gene Allison

CLIENT
Pirelli Tire Corp.

AGENCY/STUDIO
AC&R / CCL

PRODUCTION COMPANY
Anderson Litho

ART DIRECTOR
Cliff Sorah

DESIGNER
Cliff Sorah

PRODUCER
Meredith Ott

WRITER
Liz Paradise

PHOTOGRAPHER
Rob Larsen

CLIENT
Va. State Penitentiary
Creative Workshop

AGENCY/STUDIO
The Martin Agency

ART DIRECTOR
Steve Luker

PRODUCER
Deborah Wieland

WRITER
Alan Yamamoto

PHOTOGRAPHER
Dale Windham

CLIENT
Brown & Haley

AGENCY/STUDIO
McCann-Erickson

ART DIRECTOR
John Vitro

WRITERS
John Robertson
Phil Lanier

PHOTOGRAPHER
James Jannard

CLIENT
Oakley, Inc.

AGENCY/STUDIO
Chiat / Day

"PIT STOP"

SFX: Natural throughout.

ANNOUNCER VO: At Porsche, key personnel meet
on a regular basis to discuss alterations and
refinements.
At these times, many important contributions
are made in the perfecting of our cars.
We try to keep the meetings short.

ART DIRECTORS
Andy Dijak
Mas Yamashita
PRODUCER
Richard O'Neill
DIRECTOR
Eric Saarinen
WRITER
Bill Stenton
CLIENT
Porsche Cars
North America
AGENCY/STUDIO
Chiat/Day

TELEVISION-PRODUCT

ART DIRECTOR
Bob Ribits
PRODUCERS
Angelo Antonucci
Carole Floodstrand
DIRECTOR
Gerry Miller
WRITER
Alex Goslar
CLIENT
Procter & Gamble / Cheer
AGENCY/STUDIO
Leo Burnett Company

"ICE CREAM"

AUDIO: Music throughout

"HANDKERCHIEF"

AUDIO: Music throughout

ART DIRECTOR
Bob Ribits
PRODUCERS
Angelo Antonucci
Carole Floodstrand
CREATIVE DIRECTOR
Gerry Miller
CLIENT
Procter & Gamble / Cheer
AGENCY/STUDIO
Leo Burnett Company

ART DIRECTOR
Slan Blavins

PRODUCERS
Debora January/Ketchum
Japhet Asher/Colossal

DIRECTOR
George Evelyn

WRITER
Larry Kopald

PHOTOGRAPHER
Patti Stein

ILLUSTRATOR
Gary Larson

CLIENT
DHL Worldwide Express

AGENCY/STUDIO
Kethum Advertising/S.F.

PRODUCTION COMPANY
Colossal Pictures

"PIANO"

VIDEO: A caveman is carving a piano out of stone.

ANNCR: DHL presents: International shipping.

SFX: CHIPPING, PTERADACTYL SCREECH

ANNCR: Some express companies have just started to carve a niche for themselves in international shipping. But DHL has been shipping packages overseas for twenty years. You see, in international shipping, there's only one virtuoso.

SFX: KNUCKLE CRACKS

V.O.: The other guys...

SFX: BANG, BANG

V.O.:...are just learning how to play. DHL. The world's express company.

 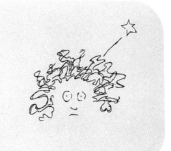 

"BAD HAIRCUT"

VIDEO: Line drawings of a woman representing the ideas the stylist has for her hair, and the eventual outcome of her visit to the hair salon.

AUDIO:

WOMAN: So I went into this fancy hair salon and asked for a trim.

The stylist said what I really needed was a "frizz."

"Listen," I said, "just a trim!"

"Then maybe a wash of color?" he said.

"Babe," I said, "half an inch off the bottom, okay?"

"As you wish," he said.

Then he scalped me.

Let me tell you, having a bad haircut is like wearing a dress you hate, every day. For months!

ANNCR: Next time, Supercuts. Because nothing grows out slower than a bad haircut.

ART DIRECTOR
Martha Anne Booth
DESIGNER
Martha Anne Booth
PRODUCER
Anna Ludoweig / FCB
Chris Whitney / Colossal
DIRECTOR
George Evelyn
WRITER
Nancy Thompson
PHOTOGRAPHER
Patti Stein
ILLUSTRATOR
George Evelyn
CLIENT
Supercuts
AGENCY/STUDIO
Foote Cone Belding / SF
PRODUCTION COMPANY
Colossal Pictures

ART DIRECTOR
Sal DeVito

PRODUCER
Rachel Novak

DIRECTOR
Mark Story

WRITER
Amy Borkowsky

CLIENT
Genesee Brewing
Company

AGENCY/STUDIO
Levine, Huntley, Schmidt
& Beaver

PRODUCTION COMPANY
Story, Piccolo, Guliner

"DOGS"

ANNOUNCER VO: This should give you some idea
of the difference between beer and Genesee
Cream Ale.
Smooth Genesee Cream Ale. It's not the same old
brewskie.

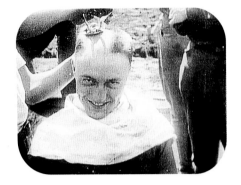

"HAIRCUTTERS FROM HELL"

ANNOUNCER VO: There are two kinds of hair-stylists in this world…
The kind that give you other cuts and the kind that give you Supercuts.
Whatever you decide, remember, your haircut should be unique, just like you.

ART DIRECTOR
Steve Stone
PRODUCER
Cindy Fluitt
DIRECTOR
Gary Johns
WRITER
Peter Wegner
CLIENT
Supercuts
AGENCY/STUDIO
Goodby, Berlin
& Silverstein
PRODUCTION COMPANY
Johns & Gorman

ART DIRECTOR
Sal DeVito

PRODUCER
Rachel Novak

DIRECTOR
Mark Story

WRITER
Amy Borkowsky

CLIENT
Genesee Brewing
Company

AGENCY/STUDIO
Levine, Huntley, Schmidt
& Beaver

PRODUCTION COMPANY
Story, Piccolo, Guliner

"DANCERS"

ANNOUNCER VO: This should give you some idea
of the difference between beer and Genesee
Cream Ale.
Smooth Genesee Cream Ale. It's not the same old
brewksie.

"LIFE CHANGES"

1967 HIPPIE: Capitalism stinks, man.
Like who needs money, man?

1973 FEMALE COLLEGE STUDENT: Beep Beep
must end. Down with the Beep.

ANNCR: Everything changes.
To stay informed of changes that affect you personally and financially read Changing Times.

1986 YUPPIE: I'm gonna get rich fast. And retire
at 35.

ANNCR: CHANGING TIMES.
Everything you and your money need to know.

ART DIRECTOR
Michael Vitiello

PRODUCER
Bob Nelson

DIRECTOR
Steve Horn

WRITER
Lee Garfinkel

CLIENT
Changing Times
Magazine

AGENCY/STUDIO
Levine, Huntley, Schmidt
& Beaver

PRODUCTION COMPANY
Steve Horn Inc.

ART DIRECTOR
Sal DeVito

PRODUCER
Rachel Novak

DIRECTOR
Mark Story

WRITER
Amy Borkowsky

CLIENT
Genesee Brewing
Company

AGENCY/STUDIO
Levine, Huntley, Schmidt
& Beaver

PRODUCTION COMPANY
Story, Piccolo, Guliner

"HORSES"

ANNOUNCER VO: This should give you some idea
of the difference between beer and Genesee
Cream Ale.
Smooth Genesee Cream Ale. It's not the same old
brewskie.

"FOREIGNER"

INTERVIEWER (off camera): Excuse me sir, are you going to run in the Examiner Bay to Breakers this year?

FOREIGNER (with accent throughout): I am a foreigner.
(Bay to Breakers music theme cuts on under all titles).

INTERVIEWER: Go.

FOREIGNER: Go, Go, Go.

INTERVIEWER: Go For It.

FOREIGNER: Go For It.
Go For It.
Go…For…It.
Go…For…It.

ART DIRECTOR
Rich Silverstein

PRODUCER
Elizabeth O'Toole

DIRECTORS
David Fowler
Robert Williamson

WRITER
David Fowler

CLIENT
Examiner Bay to Breaker

AGENCY/STUDIO
Goodby, Berlin
& Silverstein

PRODUCTION COMPANY
Robert Williamson

ART DIRECTOR
Sal DeVito

PRODUCER
Rachel Novak

DIRECTOR
Mark Story

WRITER
Amy Borkowsky

CLIENT
Genesee Brewing
Company

AGENCY/STUDIO
Levine, Huntley, Schmidt
& Beaver

PRODUCTION COMPANY
Story, Piccolo, Guliner

"BODY BUILDERS"

ANNOUNCER VO: This should give you some idea
of the difference between beer and Genesee
Cream Ale.
Smooth Genesee Cream Ale. It's not the same old
brewskie.

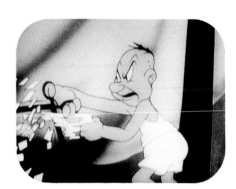

ART DIRECTOR
Steve Stone

PRODUCER
Cindy Fluitt

DIRECTOR
Gary Johns

WRITER
Peter Wegner

CLIENT
Supercuts

AGENCY/STUDIO
Goodby, Berlin
& Silverstein

PRODUCTION COMPANY
Johns & Gorman

"PUNS"

Music throughout.

ANNOUNCER VO: There are two kinds of haircuts
in this world...
Other cuts and Supercuts.
If you can't tell the difference, well, Good Luck.

TELEVISION-PRODUCT

ART DIRECTORS
Tod Seisser
Irv Klein

PRODUCER
Bob Nelson

DIRECTOR
Henry Sandbank

WRITERS
Jay Taub
Stephanie Arnold

CLIENT
Maidenform

AGENCY/STUDIO
Levine, Huntley, Schmidt
& Beaver

PRODUCTION COMPANY
Sandbank Film Prod.

"BUY TWO"

FEMALE ANNCR: I have an offer from someone
very close to you. Maidenform.
Right now, just buy any two bras, panties or lingerie styles and we'll give you another one free.
So, let's say you buy any two Maidenform bras
like these, you can get another one like this free.

SILENT SUPER: MAIDENFORM.
Buy 2 Get 1 Free
Sweet Nothings—Delectables—Chantilly

"ZOOMING KITTENS"

VIDEO: Kitten zooming around house.

V.O.: What does a frisky new kitten need? New Friskies Kitten Formula.

SFX: RACE CAR ENGINE

V.O.: Cause kittens burn up three times the energy and need three times as much calcium.

SFX: RACE CAR ENGINE

V.O.:. . as adult cats. So they need the extra protein and calcium of Friskies Kitten Formula.

SFX: RACE CAR ENGINE

V.O.: It has all the calcium of milk to build strong bones and teeth. So, if you want your frisky kitten to grow into a frisky cat, get new Friskies Kitten Formula, and bring out the frisky in your kitty.

SFX: RACE CAR ENGINE

ART DIRECTOR
Dave Mangan

DESIGNER
Dave Mangan

PRODUCER
Cindy Lee

DIRECTOR
Bruce Dorn

WRITER
Dan Seean

CLIENT
Carnation Co. Friskies

AGENCY/STUDIO
Lintas: NY

PRODUCTION COMPANY
Bruce Dorn Films

TELEVISION-PRODUCT

ART DIRECTOR
Ivan Horvath

PRODUCER
Paul Gold

ASST. PRODUCER
Trish Reeves

DIRECTOR
Joe Pytka

WRITERS
Ken Segall
Michael Baldwin

CLIENT
Apple Computer Inc.

PRODUCTION COMPANY
Pytka Productions

"THE BALANCE SHEET"

HELEN: When I fired Walters, he didn't believe it. He kept coming to work.

DEL: Helen, I just looked at these numbers. Pretty grim. Right…right here.

HELEN: I know, Del. Those are computer costs.

DEL: Didn't we pay for those systems last quarter?

HELEN: We did. But those are training costs.

DEL: Now let me get this straight. We're spending more on training than we did on the computers?

HELEN: Consultants, instructors, technical support…

DEL: But Helen, Boston doesn't show these costs.

HELEN: They use a different system.

DEL: So?

HELEN: Apparently, with their computer, their people can…train themselves.

FADE TO BLACK

DEL: Helen…doesn't that raise a question in your mind?

SUPER: Macintosh.® The power to be your best.

"WHEN A MAN LOVES A
WOMAN"   #50164

GIRL: (ON PHONE) My folks just left.

JAMES: (LOOKING UP TO THE HEAVENS).
Thank you.

ANNCR: The new Subaru Justy, gets you anywhere you want to go less expensively than any
other four wheel drive car.

JAMES: (CAUGHT OFF GUARD). Mr. Potts,
you're…home?

MR. POTTS: We turned back. The roads are
terrible.

SUPER: The new Subaru Justy.

MR. POTTS: (OVER CLOSE-UP OF JAMES) So
James, what brings you out on a night like this?

ART DIRECTOR
Michael Vitiello
PRODUCER
Bob Nelson
DIRECTOR
Steve Horn
WRITER
Lee Garfinkel
CLIENT
Subaru of America
AGENCY/STUDIO
Levine, Huntley, Schmidt
& Beaver
PRODUCTION COMPANY
Steve Horn, Inc.

ART DIRECTOR
Ivan Horvath

PRODUCERS
Paul Gold
Trish Reeves

DIRECTOR
Joe Pytka

WRITERS
Ken Segall
Michael Baldwin

CLIENT
Apple Computer Inc.

AGENCY/STUDIO
BBDO LA

PRODUCTION COMPANY
Pytka Productions

"POWER LUNCH" (:30 VERSION)

JOEY: Hey, Baldwin, how you doin'?

BALDWIN: Pretty good, Joey. How are you?

SAL: Ah, finished already.

WOMAN: Hey, I thought we were supposed to be doing this in-house.

BALDWIN: We did. New computer.

SAL: Quintile analysis? Gimme a break.

BALDWIN: Oh, Segall did that.

SAL: I thought he was in the L.A. office.

BALDWIN: Yeah, so's Edwards—she did the graphics.

SAL: So how'd you get everybody together in the same place?

BALDWIN: (UNINTELLIGIBLY) Mcntsh.

SAL: What?

BALDWIN: Mcntsh.

SAL: Pardon me?

FADE TO BLACK

SUPER: Macintosh.®

"THE WAR ROOM"

LEADER: Okay, let's get moving. First—we'll need work from every department. Who's set up for that?

IVAN: Our computers are tied in.

LEADER: Mike—how long for graphics?

MIKE: Two, three days max.

IVAN: Our computer can do it in a day.

LEADER: It's yours. Joni—typesetting and printing?

JONI: About a week, on overtime.

LEADER: Now hold on. Who published this?

IVAN: We did. On the computer.

LEADER: Well, do it again. Last, we need presentation overheads. Any ideas?

FADE TO BLACK

SUPER: Macintosh.®

ART DIRECTOR
Ivan Horvath

PRODUCERS
Paul Gold
Trish Reeves

DIRECTOR
Joe Pytka

WRITER
Ken Segall

CLIENT
Apple Computer Inc.

AGENCY/STUDIO
BBDO LA

PRODUCTION COMPANY
Pytka Productions

TELEVISION-PRODUCT

ART DIRECTOR
John Morrison

PRODUCER
Paul Gold

ASST. PRODUCER
Trish Reeves

DIRECTOR
Joe Pytka

WRITER
Robert Chandler

CLIENT
Apple Computer Inc.

AGENCY/STUDIO
BBDO LA

PRODUCTION COMPANY
Pytka Productions

"THE HOME OFFICE"

SUPER: The Home Office.

VIC: So they sent you down to check up on me?

DICK: Who am I to check up on you? *(A BEAT)*
So how's it coming?

VIC: Oh, I don't know. You tell me.

DICK: Where'd you get all this?

VIC: I keep telling you guys, the worst place to
get any work done is at work.

DICK: But you're all alone here. I mean no secre-
tary. No production department. No nothin'.

VIC: Oh, I wouldn't exactly say "nothing."

FADE TO BLACK

SUPER: Macintosh.®

"HORSES"

ANNOUNCER VO: This should give you some idea of the difference between beer and Genesee Cream Ale.
Smooth Genesee Cream Ale. It's not the same old brewskie.

ART DIRECTOR
Sal DeVito
PRODUCER
Rachel Novak
DIRECTOR
Mark Story
WRITER
Amy Borkowsky
CLIENT
Genesee Brewing
Company
AGENCY/STUDIO
Levine, Huntley, Schmidt
& Beaver
PRODUCTION COMPANY
Story, Piccolo, Guliner

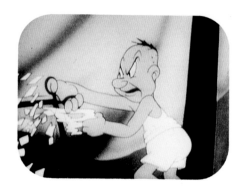

ART DIRECTOR
Steve Stone

PRODUCER
Cindy Fluitt

DIRECTOR
Gary Johns

WRITER
Peter Wegner

CLIENT
Supercuts

AGENCY/STUDIO
Goodby, Berlin
& Silverstein

PRODUCTION COMPANY
Johns & Gorman

"PUNS"

Music throughout.

ANNOUNCER VO: There are two kinds of haircuts
in this world...
Other cuts and Supercuts.
If you can't tell the difference, well, Good Luck.

OTHER CUTS

SUPERCUTS

OTHER CUTS

SUPERCUTS

SUPERCUTS

ART DIRECTOR
Steve Stone

PRODUCER
Cindy Fluitt

DIRECTOR
Gary Johns

WRITER
Peter Wegner

CLIENT
Supercuts

AGENCY/STUDIO
Goodby, Berlin
& Silverstein

PRODUCTION COMPANY
Johns & Gorman

ART DIRECTOR
Steve Stone

PRODUCER
Cindy Fluitt

DIRECTOR
Gary Johns

WRITER
Peter Wegner

CLIENT
Supercuts

AGENCY/STUDIO
Goodby, Berlin
& Silverstein

PRODUCTION COMPANY
Johns & Gorman

"TRANSFORMATIONS"

ANNOUNCER VO: There are two kinds of haircuts
in this world...
Other cuts and Supercuts.
Don't be fooled by cheap imitations.

"CELEBRITY/CHICKEN SANDWICH"

INTERVIEWER: You'd be surprised who's coming into am/pm mini markets for our new chicken sandwiches.

INTERVIEWER: Frank Felcher?

FRANK: Yeah?

INTERVIEWER: What are *you* doing here?

FRANK: Well, I *like* these hot chicken sandwiches!

KAREEM: Could I get to the mayo, buddy?

FRANK: Sure...a whole fillet of chicken breast, cooked right here, and then put on a freshly toasted bun, for just 99¢.

INTERVIEWER: 99¢?

KAREEM: Excuse me.

FRANK: Sure, pal.

KAREEM: (OC) Frank Felcher?

FRANK: So anyway, chicken's hot, tender...I come in here every day...my favorite place.

ART DIRECTOR
Ron Goodwin

PRODUCER
Len Levy

DIRECTOR
Michael Ulick

WRITER
Jocelyn Weisdorf

CLIENT
am/pm mini markets

AGENCY/STUDIO
Kresser, Craig/D.I.K.

PRODUCTION COMPANY
Ulick-Mayo Productions

Mix 'n Match Burger 'n Hot Dog, 99¢

ampm
You'd be surprised what's cookin'.

ART DIRECTOR
Ron Goodwin

PRODUCER
Len Levy

DIRECTOR
Michael Ulick

WRITER
Jocelyn Weisdorf

CLIENT
am/pm mini markets

AGENCY/STUDIO
Kresser, Craig/D.I.K.

PRODUCTION COMPANY
Ulick-Mayo Productions

"MIX-N-MATCH"

MUSIC: "DID YOU EVER HAVE TO MAKE UP YOUR MIND?" UP AND UNDER

DON KNOTTS: Should I get the hot dogs? Or the hamburgers?

ANNCR: You'd be surprised who's coming into am/pm mini markets for our Mix N' Match Special.

KNOTTS: Hamburger, great, great. Uh huh. Hot dog, terrific!

Ooh!

ANNCR: Now you can get get two Armour hot dogs. Or two 100% all-beef hamburgers. Or even one of each, done right here, for just 99¢.

KNOTTS: Okay. This is it. (TO COUNTER PERSON) I'll have a hot dog...and a hamburger.

COUNTER PERSON: Okay, sir. Would you like a bag?

KNOTTS: A bag? Uh, is there a choice? Uh, what do people...

**Burger and
Wedge cut Fries,
99¢**

ampm
**You'd be surprised
what's cookin'.**

"CELEBRITY/BURGERS-N-FRIES"

ANNCR: You'd be surprised...

...who's coming into am/pm mini markets...

...for our new fries and burger combo.

FRIDGE: (RAP A LA SUPER BOWL SHUFFLE)
A burger and fries for only ninety-nine.

For a guy like me, that's mighty fine.

Burgers real fresh, I wanna make that clear.

With new wedge fries both done right here.

Taste so good, I can't stop at one...

...at that itty-bitty price, I'm gonna get me some.
Yeah.

SFX: SOUND OF WARMER BEING REMOVED

FRIDGE: Coach might get mad...

...cuz I'm cheatin' a smidge. But what the
hey...

SFX: RAP MUSIC UP AND OUT

FRIDGE: ...gotta fill up da Fridge.

FIRST
FEDERAL

A MEMBER OF THE
1ST NATIONWIDE NETWORK

ART DIRECTORS
Jerry Gentile
Yvonne Smith

CREATIVE DIRECTORS
Pacy Markman
Bob Kuperman

PRODUCER
Shannon Silverman

DIRECTOR
Mark Story

WRITERS
Mark Monteiro
Steven Bridgewater

CLIENT
1st Nationwide Bank

AGENCY/STUDIO
DDB Needham

PRODUCTION COMPANY
Story, Piccolo, Guliner

"BREAK UP"

WOMAN #1: He was so rude to me.

...And in public, too. Then, last week, he called me by another woman's name. Bambi. Who's Bambi?

Do I look like a Bambi?

WOMAN #2: I'll take care of everything.

WOMAN #1: Would you?

ANNCR: (V.O.) At 1st Nationwide Bank we treat you with respect, concern and understanding. But don't worry. You'll get used to it.

WOMAN #2: (SPEAKING INTO PHONE)
Miss Smith will be banking with us now...

...welcome to our bank.

FIRST FEDERAL

A MEMBER OF THE
1ST NATIONWIDE NETWORK

"OUT-OF-STATE CHECK"

TELLER: Good morning, sir.

MAN: I need to cash a check.

TELLER: No problem, Mr. Bridgewater.

MAN: And I realize I'm from out of state...

TELLER: Well, your bank is part of the 1st
Nationwide Network.

MAN: (UNDER) Here's my bank card and my
license...

TELLER: That's fine, sir.

MAN: I've got 34 credit cards. Here's my passport.
This is the title to my house, title to my car, this
is the title to my favorite song...

TELLER: No, really, that's plenty.

MAN: I also belong to Joggers Anonymous. Here
are my immunization papers, my Clear Speakers
Club of America card, my one-hour photo card. I
also have a Rototillers champion card...

TELLER: (OVER) Here you go, sir.

ANNCR: (V.O.) At 1st Nationwide Bank we treat
you with respect, concern and understanding.
But don't worry. You'll get used to it.

MAN: (UNDER) .. strands of barbed wire...

ART DIRECTORS
Jerry Gentile
Yvonne Smith

CREATIVE DIRECTORS
Pacy Markman
Bob Kuperman

PRODUCER
Shannon Silverman

DIRECTOR
Mark Story

WRITERS
Mark Monteiro
Steven Bridgewater

CLIENT
1st Nationwide Bank

AGENCY/STUDIO
DDB Needham

PRODUCTION COMPANY
Story, Piccolo, Guliner

FIRST FEDERAL

A MEMBER OF THE
1ST NATIONWIDE NETWORK

ART DIRECTORS
Jerry Gentile
Yvonne Smith

CREATIVE DIRECTORS
Pacy Markman
Bob Kuperman

PRODUCER
Shannon Silverman

DIRECTOR
Mark Story

WRITERS
Mark Monteiro
Steven Bridgewater

CLIENT
1st Nationwide Bank

AGENCY/STUDIO
DDB Needham

PRODUCTION COMPANY
Story, Piccolo, Guliner

"THE LOAN"

WOMAN: Good morning. You don't remember me. I...

LOAN OFFICER: You're Miss Higgenbottham.

WOMAN: I know you see thousands of Higgenbotthams every week...

LOAN OFFICER: Yes...*(UNDER)* here it is.

WOMAN:...and a home loan has to go through many, many, many channels, and you're a busy, busy person *(UNDER)*

LOAN OFFICER: (OVER) At 1st Nationwide Bank we usually try...

WOMAN: (UNDER) ...and we all must wait...
...our turn...
...the computers are down...

LOAN OFFICER: Miss Higgenbottham.

WOMAN: I can get a third job.

LOAN OFFICER: Miss Higgenbottham.

WOMAN: Yes.

LOAN OFFICER: It's been approved.

WOMAN: That's okay. I'll come back another time.

ANNCR: (V.O.) At 1st Nationwide Bank we treat you with respect, concern and understanding. But don't worry. You'll get used to it.

"MAN"

(Music builds)

MAN: "AAAHHHHHH!"

MAN: "AAAHHHHHH!"

MAN: "AAAHHHHHH!"

(Music stops)

ANNCR: "They're only ugly until you taste 'em,
Brown & Haley Mountain Bars."

ART DIRECTOR
Steve Luker

PRODUCER
Shirley Radebaugh

WRITER
Alan Yamamoto

CLIENT
Brown & Haley

AGENCY/STUDIO
McCann-Erickson

PRODUCTION COMPANY
Third Ave. Prod.

ART DIRECTOR
Steve Luker

PRODUCER
Shirley Radebaugh

WRITER
Alan Yamamoto

CLIENT
Brown & Haley

AGENCY/STUDIO
McCann-Erickson

PRODUCTION COMPANY
Third Ave. Prod.

"TRIO"

(Music builds)

TRIO: "AAAHHHHHH!"

TRIO: "AAAHHHHHH!"

TRIO: "AAAHHHHHH!"

(Music stops)

ANNCR: "They're only ugly until you taste 'em,
Brown & Haley Mountain Bars."

"WOMAN"

(Music builds)

WOMAN: "AAAHHHHHH!"

WOMAN: "AAAHHHHHH!"

WOMAN: "AAAHHHHHH!"

(Music stops)

ANNCR: "They're only ugly until you taste 'em,
Brown & Haley Mountain Bars."

ART DIRECTOR
Steve Luker

PRODUCER
Shirley Radebaugh

WRITER
Alan Yamamoto

CLIENT
Brown & Haley

AGENCY/STUDIO
McCann-Erickson

PRODUCTION COMPANY
Third Ave. Prod.

ART DIRECTOR
Ron Fisher

PRODUCER
Rick Benson

DIRECTOR
Jerry Collamer

WRITER
Virgil Shutze

CLIENT
South Carolina Federal

AGENCY/STUDIO
Hutcheson-Shutze

PRODUCTION COMPANY
Ackerman-Benson

"ORANGUTAN"

MVO: How does your bank react when you ask for a home equity loan?

ORANGUTAN: YAWNS…

MVO: All day banking?

ORANGUTAN: SHAKES HIS HEAD NO…

MVO: Free checking?

ORANGUTAN: BLOWS A "RASPBERRY"…

MVO: How about a mortgage loan?

ORANGUTAN: SHAKES HIS HEAD NO…

MVO: Line of credit?

ORANGUTAN: STICKS OUT HIS TONGUE…

MVO: Won't even listen, ugh?

ORANGUTAN: COVERS EARS WITH HANDS…

MVO: Bet they don't even know your name?

ORANGUTAN: SHAKES HIS HEAD NO…

MVO: Must drive you clean out of your tree?

ORANGUTAN: SLAPS HANDS OVER FACE…

MVO: Well…if we were you pal, we'd bank with us.

"JOHNSON GENERATOR" ("TREADMILL")

ANNCR: We're here talking to Joshua Johnson who's just invented an alternative to the water heater. So, what prompted this creative venture, Mr. Johnson?

MAN: My water heater broke, actually.

ANNCR: Oh, I see. So you decided to invent. . . .

MAN: The Johnson generator.

ANNCR: Aha, what's its main source of power for it?

MAN: Well, here, I'll show you.
(SFX: DOOR OPENING. SOUND OF PEOPLE RUN-NING ON A TREADMILL.) What do you think?

INTERVIEWER: Oh, my! How does your family keep up that pace on that treadmill there?

MAN: Oh, they're used to it. Just wave guys! You see, it cuts down their wind if they have to talk. Pick up those feet, Jimmy! You too, Judy! Daddy's watching!

Kids. You gotta love 'em.

INTER: Have you ever thought about renting a hot water heater from Puget Power?

MAN: I think the wife mentioned that. 'Course it's hard to understand her these days, she's always out of breath.

INTER: A few dollars a month is really all it takes. They'll install it and if it ever needs it, fix it for free. Just call 1-800-421-RENT.

MAN: By golly, I'll do that. Here, jump on this bicycle and start peddling.

ANNCR: Why?

MAN: Powers the phone.

ANNCR: To rent or buy an energy-efficient water heater, call 1-800-421-RENT. Puget Power. The energy starts here.
(SFX: *FRANTIC PACE OF BICYCLE.*)

MAN: C'mon, get those legs working will ya, it's long distance.

ANNCR: I'm tryin'!

MAN: Hello? Pump harder!

ANNCR: I'm tryin'!

MAN: Hello? Can you hear me?

"FLAME THROWER"

INTERVIEWER: So Mr. Wandermaker. How does it feel to hold the record for the world's oldest water heater?

MR: Cold. Ha! A little water heater humor. Actually, it doesn't really heat water anymore, so I've had to resort to other means.

INTER: Like what?

MR: This!

INTER: Isn't that a flame thrower?

MR: It's the quickest way I know to heat water. Here. Let me show you.

MR: (SFX: THE WHOOSH OF FIRE. CAT: Meowwww!!)
Ooops! Sorry kitten!

INTER: You know, there is an easier way.

MR: But I'm finally getting the hang of this, one more try. *(SFX: WHOOSH. CAT:* Meowww!)
Ooops.

INTER: A few dollars a month is all it costs to rent a water heater from Puget Power. They even have a program for people who want to own.

MR: Gee, that is cheap. But can it light a candelabra from 30 feet away? *(SFX: WHOOSH.)*

INTER: Look, Puget Power can install it for free, maintain it for free and if it ever needs it, fix it for free. Just call 1-800-421-RENT for details.

MR: Okay, you sold me. Now listen, why don't you stay for dinner. We're having a barbecue.

INTER: A barbecue? I didn't see a barbecue?

MR: Don't need one with this baby. Hope you like 'em well done! *(SFX: WHOOOSH!!)*

ANNCR: To rent or own an energy-efficient state-of-the-art water heater, just call 1-800-421-RENT. Puget Power. The energy starts here.

MR: (SFX: WHOOOSH!! CAT: Meooowww!!) Oh gee, sorry Felix, boy can he move, huh.

RADIO

PRODUCER
Shirley Radebaugh
WRITER
Alan Yamamoto
CLIENT
Puget Power
AGENCY/STUDIO
McCann-Erickson
PRODUCTION COMPANY
Griffiths, Gibson
& Ramsay

RADIO

PRODUCER
Shirley Radebaugh

WRITER
Alan Yamamoto

CLIENT
Puget Power

AGENCY/STUDIO
McCann-Erickson

PRODUCTION COMPANY
Griffiths, Gibson
& Ramsay

PRODUCER
Rich Peterson

DIRECTOR
Rich Peterson

WRITERS
Neal Howard
David Begler

CLIENT
Hamilton Beach

AGENCY/STUDIO
Sound Patrol

PRODUCTION COMPANY
Rich Peterson

"HOT ROCKS"

INTERVIEWER: We're talking to Mr. Anderson who is, at this moment, sitting in his bathtub. *(SFX: WATER SPLASHING SOUNDS.)*

MR: Now you're sure this is radio? Not TV?

INTER: It's radio, Mr. Anderson, don't worry. Now, you've come up with an alternative to getting hot bath water since your hot water heater broke back in 1965, I understand.

MR: Well, that's right. Here, I'll show you how it works. Okay Snookums! Bring 'em in!

You see, first, we heat these rocks in the oven and. . . .

MRS: Coming through! Hot rocks!

MR: This is the only part that takes a little getting used . . . *(SFX: SPLASH! SIZZLING OF WATER.)*

. . . TOOOOO OOOW!! *(SCREAMS)* WHAAAHHHH!!

MR: Oh, I love it when she does that.

INTER: Why didn't you just rent or buy a water heater from Puget Power?

MR: Well, we had all these rocks in the backyard and I just thought . . .

INTER: For a few dollars a month, you can have all the hot water you need.

MR: You mean no more hot rocks?

INTER: That's right. Puget Power can install it for free, maintain it for free and if it ever needs it, fix it for free. Just call 1-800-421-RENT for details.

MR: Boy! That sounds great. I got to tell the wife. Hey Honey!

MRS: Water's cold dear? Here you go. *(SFX: SPLASHING OF ROCKS, SIZZLING WATER.)*

MR: WHHHHAAAA!!!!

ANNCR: To rent or own an energy-efficient, state-of-the-art water heater, just call 1-800-421-RENT. Puget Power. The energy starts here.

MR: I love it when she does that.

ANNCR: Yeah.

"BEEP"

SFX: (BEEP) WHERE INDICATED

ANNCR: During the next 50 seconds of this commercial for the new Hamilton Beach Scorch Guard Iron with the no-scorch beeper, if you hear *BEEP* it's not because we're being censored for saying anything bad like "son of a *BEEP*" or "you *BEEP*" or "*BEEP* yours."

It's simply an audible warning from the Hamilton Beach Scorch Guard Iron that you're about to burn the *BEEP* out of your *BEEP*ing shirt. You see, the Hamilton Beach Scorch Guard Iron has a built-in sensor that goes *BEEP* after 8 seconds if you've left the hot iron on your clothes too long. What's even more amazing is that after ironing, if you leave the Hamilton Beach Scorch Guard on in the upright position, it will *BEEP* after 8 minutes to remind you to turn it off. And that's no bull*BEEP*.

So the next time you get distracted from your ironing, let's say because the *BEEP*ing phone keeps ringing off the *BEEP*ing hook, don't worry, you won't scorch your clothes, because you'll have the Hamilton Beach Scorch Guard Iron with the built-in electronic sensor that goes *BEEP*. Again, that's not like a moral censor that goes *BEEP*, but the kind of sensor that goes *BEEP*. Well, you know what I mean.

(ASIDE) Can I get the *BEEP* out of here now?

"CHOY MUN JERN"

ANNCR: Choy Mun Jern, visiting dignitary from the People's Republic of China.

(MAN SPEAKING CHINESE UNDER THROUGHOUT)

TRANSLATOR: (A WOMAN'S VOICE WITH HINT OF BRITISH ACCENT)

I'd like please to thank you . . . for this shiny opportunity . . . to become . . . plastic fruit.

Your country is happy . . . like a sheep . . . with its head . . . stuck in a fence.

For sure . . . it is a monkey wrench.

The people fill me . . . with a great . . . reluctance. We are all . . . we are all percolators.

ANNCR: What's Mr. Choy really saying? Cross-cultural confusion is just one reason why the San Francisco Examiner will soon open three news bureaus in the Pacific Rim. The only Bay Area paper to do so in Tokyo, Seoul and Beijing. Prize-winning journalists will report news of the Far East clearly and comprehensively. From the next generation at the Examiner.

(CHINESE-SPEAKING MAN RESUMES)

TRANSLATOR: Finally, I would like to say . . . I admire . . . your stupid haircut . . . Thank-you many buckets.

RADIO

CREATIVE DIRECTOR
Rich Silverstein
PRODUCER
Robin Olesen
WRITER
Peter Wegner
CLIENT
S.F. Newspaper Agency
AGENCY/STUDIO
Goodby, Berlin
& Silverstein
PRODUCTION COMPANY
TLA Productions

RADIO

PRODUCER
Shirley Radebaugh

WRITER
Alan Yamamoto

CLIENT
Puget Power

AGENCY/STUDIO
McCann-Erickson

PRODUCTION COMPANY
Griffiths, Gibson
& Ramsay

"FLAME THROWER"

INTERVIEWER: So Mr. Wandermaker. How does it feel to hold the record for the world's oldest water heater?

MR: Cold. Ha! A little water heater humor. Actually, it doesn't really heat water anymore, so I've had to resort to other means.

INTER: Like what?

MR: This!

INTER: Isn't that a flame thrower?

MR: It's the quickest way I know to heat water. Here. Let me show you.

MR: (SFX: THE WHOOSH OF FIRE. CAT: Meowwww!!)
Ooops! Sorry kitten!

INTER: You know, there is an easier way.

MR: But I'm finally getting the hang of this, one more try. *(SFX: WHOOSH. CAT:* Meowww!) Ooops.

INTER: A few dollars a month is all it costs to rent a water heater from Puget Power. They even have a program for people who want to own.

MR: Gee, that is cheap. But can it light a candelabra from 30 feet away? *(SFX: WHOOSH.)*

INTER: Look, Puget Power can install it for free, maintain it for free and if it ever needs it, fix it for free. Just call 1-800-421-RENT for details.

MR: Okay, you sold me. Now listen, why don't you stay for dinner. We're having a barbecue.

INTER: A barbecue? I didn't see a barbecue?

MR: Don't need one with this baby. Hope you like 'em well done! *(SFX: WHOOOSH!!)*

ANNCR: To rent or own an energy-efficient state-of-the-art water heater, just call 1-800-421-RENT. Puget Power. The energy starts here.

MR: (SFX: WHOOOSH!! CAT: Meooowww!!) Oh gee, sorry Felix, boy can he move, huh.

"JOHNSON GENERATOR"
("TREADMILL")

ANNCR: We're here talking to Joshua Johnson who's just invented an alternative to the water heater. So, what prompted this creative venture, Mr. Johnson?

MAN: My water heater broke, actually.

ANNCR: Oh, I see. So you decided to invent. . . .

MAN: The Johnson generator.

ANNCR: Aha, what's its main source of power for it?

MAN: Well, here, I'll show you.
(SFX: DOOR OPENING. SOUND OF PEOPLE RUNNING ON A TREADMILL.) What do you think?

INTERVIEWER: Oh, my! How does your family keep up that pace on that treadmill there?

MAN: Oh, they're used to it. Just wave guys! You see, it cuts down their wind if they have to talk. Pick up those feet, Jimmy! You too, Judy! Daddy's watching!

Kids. You gotta love 'em.

INTER: Have you ever thought about renting a hot water heater from Puget Power?

MAN: I think the wife mentioned that. 'Course it's hard to understand her these days, she's always out of breath.

INTER: A few dollars a month is really all it takes. They'll install it and if it ever needs it, fix it for free. Just call 1-800-421-RENT.

MAN: By golly, I'll do that. Here, jump on this bicycle and start peddling.

ANNCR: Why?

MAN: Powers the phone.

ANNCR: To rent or buy an energy-efficient water heater, call 1-800-421-RENT. Puget Power. The energy starts here.
(SFX: FRANTIC PACE OF BICYCLE.)

MAN: C'mon, get those legs working will ya, it's long distance.

ANNCR: I'm tryin'!

MAN: Hello? Pump harder!

ANNCR: I'm tryin'!

MAN: Hello? Can you hear me?

"HOT ROCKS"

INTERVIEWER: We're talking to Mr. Anderson who is, at this moment, sitting in his bathtub. *(SFX: WATER SPLASHING SOUNDS.)*

MR: Now you're sure this is radio? Not TV?

INTER: It's radio, Mr. Anderson, don't worry. Now, you've come up with an alternative to getting hot bath water since your hot water heater broke back in 1965, I understand.

MR: Well, that's right. Here, I'll show you how it works. Okay Snookums! Bring 'em in!

You see, first, we heat these rocks in the oven and. . . .

MRS: Coming through! Hot rocks!

MR: This is the only part that takes a little getting used . . . *(SFX: SPLASH! SIZZLING OF WATER.)*

. . .TOOOOO OOOW!! *(SCREAMS)* WHAAAHHHH!!

MR: Oh, I love it when she does that.

INTER: Why didn't you just rent or buy a water heater from Puget Power?

MR: Well, we had all these rocks in the backyard and I just thought . . .

INTER: For a few dollars a month, you can have all the hot water you need.

MR: You mean no more hot rocks?

INTER: That's right. Puget Power can install it for free, maintain it for free and if it ever needs it, fix it for free. Just call 1-800-421-RENT for details.

MR: Boy! That sounds great. I got to tell the wife. Hey Honey!

MRS: Water's cold dear? Here you go. *(SFX: SPLASHING OF ROCKS, SIZZLING WATER.)*

MR: WHHHHAAAA!!!!

ANNCR: To rent or own an energy-efficient, state-of-the-art water heater, just call 1-800-421-RENT. Puget Power. The energy starts here.

MR: I love it when she does that.

ANNCR: Yeah.

"RAW RAP"

RAPPERS: CHECK IT OUT, PARTY PEOPLE IN THE PLACE TO BE
LET ME TELL YOU 'BOUT A MOVIE THAT YOU GOTTA SEE
EDDIE MURPHY RAW, EDDIE MURPHY LIVE
HE'S RAW . . . R-R-RAW

EDDIE: LAUGHS

RAPPERS: EDDIE MURPHY RAW, THAT'S THE NAME OF THIS FLICK
SO GET YOUR TICKETS AND GET 'EM QUICK . . . QU-QU-QUICK
'COS THE WAY MY MAN EDDIE'S GONNA ROCK THE SPOT
YOU KNOW THERE'S GONNA BE LINES AROUND THE BLOCK
HE'S RAW . . . R-R-RAW

STRAIGHT OUT, UN CUT, NO CENSORS ALLOWED
EDDIE'S RAW AND EDDIE'S PROUD
THIS IS THE MOVIE YOU'VE BEEN WAITING FOR
SO DON'T MISS EDDIE MURPHY RAW
RAW, RAW, RAW . . . *(ETC)*

EDDIE: *(LAUGHTER)* "C'mon, that's the way I like it . . . I like it . . . I like it, I like it, I like it!"

ANNCR: *EDDIE MURPHY RAW* THE MOVIE FROM PARAMOUNT, RATED R

AUDIENCE: APPLAUSE

PRODUCER
Shirley Radebaugh
WRITER
Alan Yamamoto
CLIENT
Puget Power
AGENCY/STUDIO
McCann-Erickson
PRODUCTION COMPANY
Griffiths, Gibson
& Ramsay

RADIO

PRODUCERS
Paul Wales
Smitty
DIRECTOR
Steve Proffitt
WRITER
Steve Proffitt
CLIENT
Nancy Goliger
AGENCY/STUDIO
Paramount Pictures

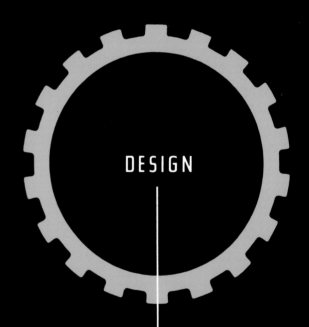

DESIGN

ANNUAL REPORT

ART DIRECTOR
Kit Hinrichs

DESIGNERS
Kit Hinrichs
Lenore Bartz

WRITER
Delphine Hirasuna

PHOTOGRAPHERS
Tom Tracy
Barry Robinson

ILLUSTRATORS
Doug Smith
Mark Summers
Max Seabaugh
Dave Stevenson

CLIENT
Potlatch Corporation

AGENCY/STUDIO
Pentagram Design

ART DIRECTOR
Stephen Ferrari

DESIGNER
Amy Knoell-Watson

CLIENT
Seamen's Corporation

AGENCY/STUDIO
The Graphic Expression

ART DIRECTOR
Robert Miles Runyan

DESIGNER
Michael Mescall

PHOTOGRAPHER
Cynthia Moore

CLIENT
Columbia Savings
& Loan

AGENCY/STUDIO
Robert Miles Runyan
& Associates

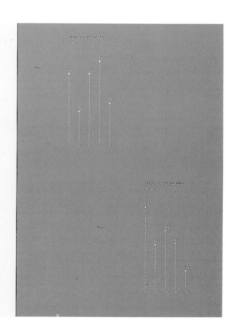

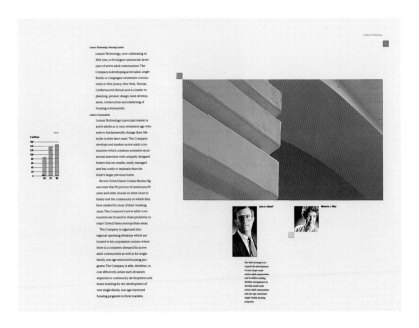

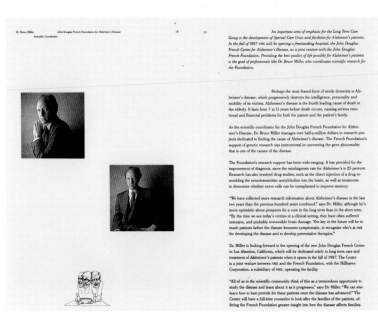

ANNUAL REPORT

ART DIRECTOR
Gary Hinsche

DESIGNER
Gary Hinsche

PHOTOGRAPHERS
Scott Morgan
Lonnie Duka

CLIENT
Leisure Technology

AGENCY/STUDIO
Robert Miles Runyan
& Associates

ART DIRECTOR
Jim Berté

DESIGNER
Jim Berté

WRITER
Tiuu Luuk

PHOTOGRAPHER
William Coupon

ILLUSTRATOR
Martin Ledyard

CLIENT
National Medical
Enterprises, Inc.

AGENCY/STUDIO
Robert Miles Runyan
& Associates

ART DIRECTOR
Hershell George

DESIGNER
Hershell George

WRITER
Shelley Mazor

PHOTOGRAPHERS
Nelson Bakerman
Dan Kozan

CLIENT
Shorewood Packaging
Corporation

AGENCY/STUDIO
Hershell George Graphics

ANNUAL REPORT

ART DIRECTOR
Ron Jefferies

DESIGNER
Susan Garland

WRITER
Ron Bissell

PHOTOGRAPHER
Russ Widstrand

CLIENT
Fluorocarbon Company

AGENCY/STUDIO
The Jefferies Association

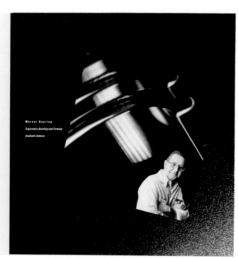

ART DIRECTORS
Ken White
Mike Ward

DESIGNERS
Ken White
Dan Ahn

WRITER
Kerry Lamperts

PHOTOGRAPHER
Eric Myer

CLIENT
Pacific Financial
Companies

AGENCY/STUDIO
White + Associates

ART DIRECTOR
Robert Appleton

DESIGNER
Robert Appleton

WRITER
Edwin Simon

PHOTOGRAPHER
Costa Manos/Magnum

CLIENT
The Advest Group Inc.

AGENCY/STUDIO
Appleton Design Inc.

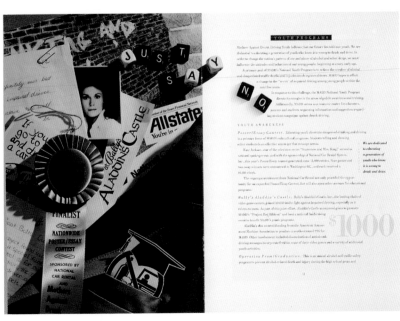

ANNUAL REPORT

ART DIRECTORS
Douglas Joseph
Rik Besser

DESIGNER
Douglas Joseph

WRITER
Dick Hoffman

PHOTOGRAPHER
Burton Pritzker

CLIENT
Dep Corporation

AGENCY/STUDIO
Besser Joseph Partners

ART DIRECTOR
Bryan L. Peterson

DESIGNER
Bryan L. Peterson

WRITER
Steve Lawrence

PHOTOGRAPHER
Paul Talley

CLIENT
Mothers Against
Drunk Driving

AGENCY/STUDIO
Peterson & Company

ART DIRECTORS
Peter Harrison
Harold Burch

DESIGNERS
Harold Burch
Peter Harrison

WRITER
Les Edwards

PHOTOGRAPHER
Scott Morgan

ILLUSTRATOR
John Van Hammersveld

CLIENT
Warner
Communications Inc.

AGENCY/STUDIO
Pentagram

▲

ANNUAL REPORT

ART DIRECTOR
Stephen Ferrari

DESIGNER
Stephen Ferrari

PHOTOGRAPHERS
Terry Heffernan
William Taufic

CLIENT
Dillon Read & Co. Inc.

AGENCY/STUDIO
The Graphic Expression

ART DIRECTOR
John Van Dyke

DESIGNER
John Van Dyke

DIRECTOR
John Van Dyke

WRITER
Stuart Clugston

PHOTOGRAPHERS
Chris Weigel
Howard Fry
Terry Heffern

CLIENT
B.C.F.P.

AGENCY/STUDIO
Van Dyke Company

ART DIRECTORS
Pat Samata
Greg Samata

DESIGNERS
Pat Samata
Greg Samata

WRITER
Joel Feldstein

PHOTOGRAPHER
Mark Joseph

ILLUSTRATORS
Ann Teson
K.C. Yoon

CLIENT
Leaf Inc.

AGENCY/STUDIO
Samata Associates

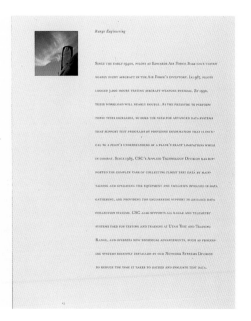

ANNUAL REPORT

ART DIRECTOR
Robert Miles Runyan

DESIGNER
Michael Mescall

WRITER
Computer Sciences Corp.

PHOTOGRAPHER
Scott Morgan

CLIENT
Computer Sciences Corp.

AGENCY/STUDIO
Robert Miles Runyan
& Associates

ART DIRECTOR
Kit Hinrichs

DESIGNERS
Kit Hinrichs
Karen Berndt

WRITER
Maxine Gaiber

PHOTOGRAPHERS
Steven A. Heller (Cover)
Barry Robinson
(Back Cover)

ILLUSTRATORS
Michael Schwab
Doug Boyd

CLIENT
Art Center College
of Design

AGENCY/STUDIO
Pentagram Design

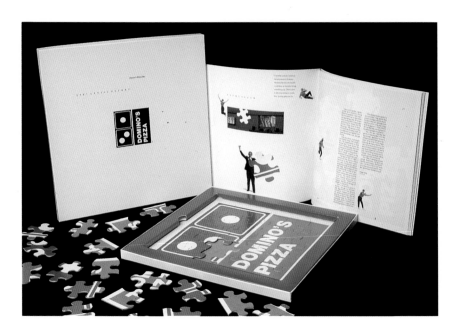

ART DIRECTOR
Ernie Perich

DESIGNERS
Carol Austin
Carol Mooradian
Tom Masters
Gary Bastien
Janine Thielk

WRITER
Linda Fitzgerald

PHOTOGRAPHER
Tony Segielski

CLIENT
Domino's Pizza, Inc.

AGENCY/STUDIO
Perich Partners, Ltd.

ANNUAL REPORT

ART DIRECTOR
David Broom

DESIGNER
Kimiko Murakami Chan

WRITER
California Casualty
Group

PHOTOGRAPHERS
Henry Gilpin
Brett Weston
Paul Caponigro
Ray McSavaney

ADDITIONAL
PHOTOGRAPHERS
Howard Bond
Bruce Barnbaum
Stu Levy
Curt Fischer

CLIENT
California Casualty
Group

AGENCY/STUDIO
Broom & Broom

ART DIRECTOR
Ronald Morris

DESIGNERS
Ronald Morris
Paul Ison

WRITER
Bay Pacific

PHOTOGRAPHERS
Steve Williams
4x5 (Stock)

CLIENT
Bay Pacific Health
Corporation

AGENCY/STUDIO
Delmatoff Gerow Morris
Langhans

ART DIRECTOR
Lawrence Bender

DESIGNER
Margaret
Hellmann Cheu

WRITER
Melanie McNulty

PHOTOGRAPHER
Geoffrey Nelson

ILLUSTRATOR
Margaret
Hellmann Cheu

CLIENT
Scientific Micro
Systems, Inc.

AGENCY/STUDIO
Lawrence Bender
& Associates

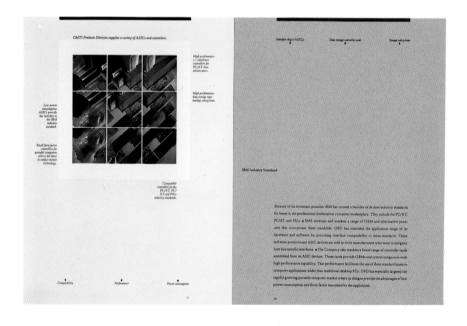

BROCHURE, FOLDER

ART DIRECTOR
Robert Miles Runyan

DESIGNER
Edie Garrett

WRITER
Obunsha Corp.

PHOTOGRAPHER
Various

CLIENT
Obunsha Corp.

AGENCY/STUDIO
Robert Miles Runyan
& Associates

ART DIRECTOR
Cheryl Heller

DESIGNERS
Cheryl Heller
David Lopes

WRITER
Peter Caroline

PHOTOGRAPHER
Clint Clemens

CLIENT
S.D. Warren

AGENCY/STUDIO
Heller Breene

ART DIRECTORS
Barry Shepard
Douglas Reeder

DESIGNERS
Douglas Reeder
Steve Ditko

WRITER
Steve Hogan

PHOTOGRAPHER
Rick Rusing

ILLUSTRATOR
Roland Dahlquist

CLIENT
Audi of America, Inc.

AGENCY/STUDIO
SHR Design
Communications

BROCHURE, FOLDER

ART DIRECTORS
David Edelstein
Nancy Edelstein
Lanny French

DESIGNERS
David Edelstein
Nancy Edelstein
Lanny French
Carol Davidson

PRODUCER
D. Thom Bissett

WRITER
Kathy Cain

PHOTOGRAPHER
Peter Gravelle

CLIENT
Generra Sportswear

AGENCY/STUDIO
Edelstein Associates
▲

DESIGNER
Peter Richards

WRITER
Brian McKenna

PHOTOGRAPHER
Langley Penoyar

CLIENT
Nike

AGENCY/STUDIO
The Richards Co.

ART DIRECTOR
Michael Cronan

DESIGNERS
Michael Cronan
Roz Romney

WRITER
Stacey Bovero

PHOTOGRAPHER
Thomas Heinser

CLIENT
Levi Strauss & Co.

AGENCY/STUDIO
Cronan Design

BROCHURE, FOLDER

ART DIRECTOR
Michael Cronan

DESIGNERS
M. Cronan
S. Fukutome

PHOTOGRAPHER
Thomas Heinser

CLIENT
Levi Strauss & Co.

AGENCY/STUDIO
Cronan Design

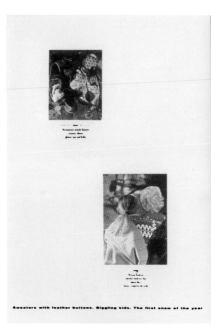

ART DIRECTOR
Joanne Biron

DESIGNER
Joanne Biron

WRITER
Linda Satterfield

CLIENT
Boston Traders

AGENCY/STUDIO
Heller Breene

▲

ART DIRECTORS
David Edelstein
Lanny French

DESIGNERS
David Edelstein
Lanny French
Carol Davidson

WRITER
Kathy Cain

PHOTOGRAPHER
Ben Kerns

CLIENT
Code Bleu Sportswear

AGENCY/STUDIO
Edelstein Associates

BROCHURE, FOLDER

ART DIRECTOR
Carole Bouchard

DESIGNER
Carole Bouchard

WRITER
Linda Satterfield

PHOTOGRAPHER
Phil Porcella

CLIENT
Hospice

AGENCY/STUDIO
Heller Breene
▲

BOB CONGE   SEYMOUR CHWAST

ART DIRECTOR
Kenneth Carbone

DESIGNER
Eric Pike

CLIENT
HTI Visual

AGENCY/STUDIO
Carbone Smolan
Associates

ART DIRECTOR
Gary Hinsche

DESIGNER
Gary Hinsche

PHOTOGRAPHER
Robert Stevens
Photography

CLIENT
George Rice & Sons

AGENCY/STUDIO
Robert Miles Runyan
& Associates

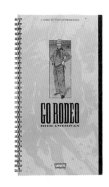

BROCHURE, FOLDER

ART DIRECTOR
Neal Zimmermann
LS&Co.

DESIGNERS
Dennis Crowe
Neal Zimmerman

ILLUSTRATOR
Dennis Crowe

CLIENT
Levi Strauss & Co.

AGENCY/STUDIO
Belew Design

PRINTER
Atomic Press
▲

ART DIRECTORS
James Cross
Jay Novak

DESIGNER
Joseph Jacquez

PHOTOGRAPHERS
Disney In-House
Charles Imstepf
Warren Faubel

ILLUSTRATOR
Disney In-House

CLIENT
Euro Disneyland

AGENCY/STUDIO
Cross Associates

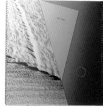

ART DIRECTOR
John Coy

DESIGNERS
John Coy
Richard Atkins
Tom Bauman

PHOTOGRAPHER
Jim McHugh

CLIENT
Newport Harbor
Art Museum

AGENCY/STUDIO
Coy, Los Angeles

PRINTER
Typecraft, Inc.

BROCHURE, FOLDER

ART DIRECTORS
Peslak/Wolkenberg

DESIGNERS
Peslak/Wolkenberg

WRITER
Iris Demauro

PHOTOGRAPHER
Victor Schrager

CLIENT
Geo International

AGENCY/STUDIO
Platium Design, Inc.

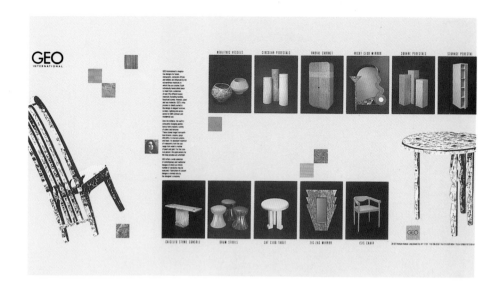

ART DIRECTOR
Ron Manzke

DESIGNER
Douglas Lloyd

CLIENT
Wordmark/NY

AGENCY/STUDIO
Landor Associates
▲

ART DIRECTOR
Linda Warren

DESIGNER
Linda Warren

WRITER
Karen Bram

ILLUSTRATOR
Andrzej Dudzinski

CLIENT
Anaheim Memorial
Hospital

AGENCY/STUDIO
Communications Plus

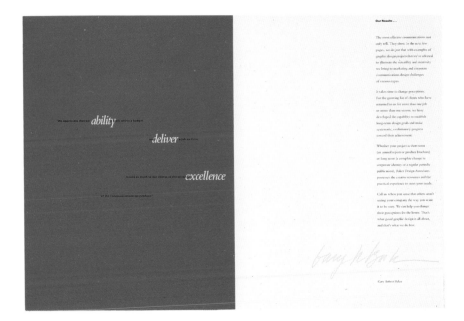

BROCHURE, FOLDER

ART DIRECTOR
Gary R. Baker

DESIGNERS
Gary R. Baker
Vicki Adjami

WRITER
Victoria Branch

PHOTOGRAPHER
Scott Slobodian

AGENCY/STUDIO
Baker Design Associates
▲

ART DIRECTOR
David Arthur Hadlock

DESIGNER
David Arthur Hadlock

CLIENT
Ron Loosen
Associates Design

BROCHURE, FOLDER

ART DIRECTOR
Stephen Ferrari

DESIGNER
Amy Knoell Watson

PHOTOGRAPHER
Jim Barber

CLIENT
Phibro Energy, Inc.

AGENCY/STUDIO
The Graphic Expression

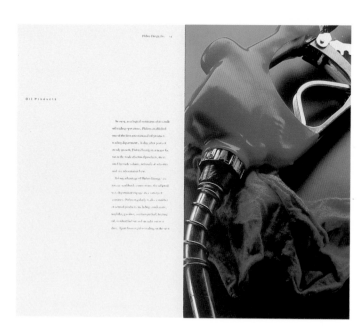

ART DIRECTOR
John T. Cleveland

DESIGNER
John T. Cleveland

WRITER
Rose DeNeve

PHOTOGRAPHER
Various

ILLUSTRATOR
Various

CLIENT
S.D. Warren

AGENCY/STUDIO
John Cleveland, Inc.

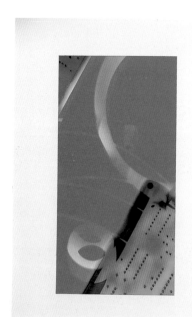

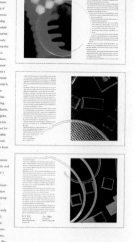

ART DIRECTOR
Barry Shepard

DESIGNERS
Barry Shepard
Steve Ditko
Karin Burklein Arnold
Douglas Reeder

WRITER
Steve Hogan

PHOTOGRAPHERS
Rick Rusing
Rick Gayle

ILLUSTRATORS
Rolland Dahlquist
Rick Kirkman

CLIENT
Audi of America, Inc.

AGENCY/STUDIO
SHR Design
Communications

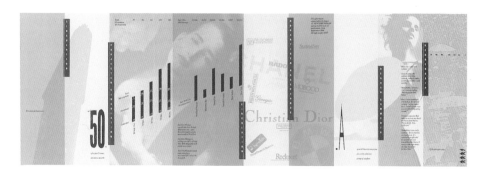

BROCHURE, FOLDER

DESIGNER
Peter Richards

WRITER
Tom McCarthy

PHOTOGRAPHERS
Langley Penoyar
Chuck Kuhn
Bill Cannon
Kelly Povo

ILLUSTRATORS
George Abe
Kriten Knutson

CLIENT
Rainier Color

AGENCY/STUDIO
The Richards Co.

DESIGNER
John Van Dyke

PHOTOGRAPHER
Terry Heffernan

CLIENT
Weyerhaeuser Paper

AGENCY/STUDIO
Samata Design

ART DIRECTOR
John T. Parham

DESIGNER
Eric Spillman

CLIENT
New York Woman
Magazine (Amy Krakow)

AGENCY/STUDIO
Parham-Santana Inc.

BROCHURE, FOLDER

ART DIRECTOR
David Carter

DESIGNER
Gary Lobue, Jr.

ILLUSTRATOR
Gary Lobue, Jr.

CLIENT
The Catamaran Motel

AGENCY/STUDIO
David Carter Design

3-D PACKAGING

ART DIRECTOR
Benjamin Cziller

DESIGNER
Benjamin Cziller

CLIENT
Footsie

AGENCY/STUDIO
Cziller Design

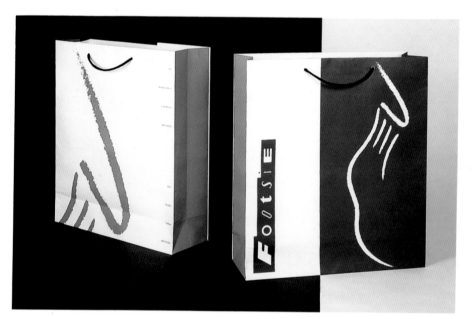

ART DIRECTORS
Jon Reeder
Tom Binnion

DESIGNERS
Jon Reeder
Tom Binnion

WRITERS
Tom Binnion
Jon Reeder

CLIENT
Off Center Corporation

AGENCY/STUDIO
Thomas Binnion/
Jon Reeder

3-D PACKAGING

ART DIRECTOR
Mark Oliver
DESIGNERS
Mark Oliver
Jay Boettner
CLIENT
Firestone & Fletcher
Brewing Co.
AGENCY/STUDIO
Mark Oliver, Inc.

ART DIRECTOR
Mitchell Mauk
DESIGNER
Mitchell Mauk
TYPOGRAPHER
Z Typography
PHOTOGRAPHER
Rick Eskite
CLIENT
Amdek Inc.
AGENCY/STUDIO
Metaphor
PRODUCTION COMPANY
Curry Signs Inc.

3-D PACKAGING

ART DIRECTORS
Thom Marchionna
Tim Brennan
Stephen Sieler

DESIGNER
Stephen Sieler

WRITER
Thom Marchionna

ILLUSTRATOR
Jose Ortega

AGENCY/STUDIO
Apple Creative Services

ART DIRECTOR
Jennifer Morla

DESIGNER
Jennifer Morla

WRITER
Alice Medrich

CLIENT
Cocolat

AGENCY/STUDIO
Morla Design, Inc.

SALES KIT, PRESS KIT

ART DIRECTORS
Jim Cross
Ken Cook

DESIGNER
Ken Cook

WRITER
Judith Kermeen

PHOTOGRAPHER
Steve Underwood

ILLUSTRATOR
Randy South

CLIENT
Simpson Paper Company

AGENCY/STUDIO
Cross Associates
▲

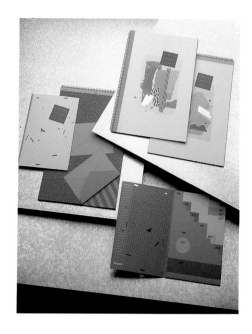

HOUSE ORGAN,
NEWSLETTER

ART DIRECTOR
Kit Hinrichs

DESIGNERS
Kit Hinrichs
Lenore Bartz

WRITERS
Susan Hoffman
Jean Keefe Parry

PHOTOGRAPHERS
Steven A. Heller
Henrik Kam (cover)

ILLUSTRATORS
John Mattos
Walid Saba

CLIENT
Art Center
College of Design

AGENCY/STUDIO
Pentagram Design

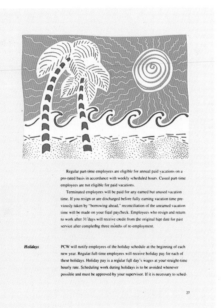

ART DIRECTOR
Diane Gromala

DESIGNERS
Diane Gromala
Kathy Warinner

WRITERS
Janet McGinnis
Shelley Ginenthel

ILLUSTRATOR
Kathy Warinner

CLIENT
PCW Communications

AGENCY/STUDIO
In-House

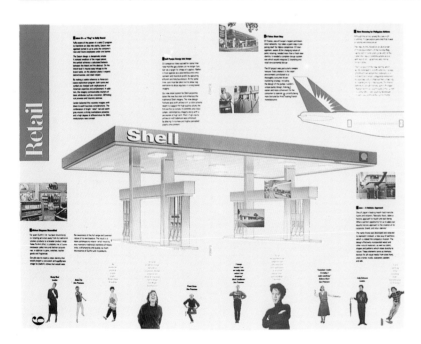

ART DIRECTOR
Landor Design Team

DESIGNER
Landor Design Team

WRITER
Landor Staff

PHOTOGRAPHER
Landor Photography
Studio

CLIENT
Landor Associates

AGENCY/STUDIO
Landor Associates

POSTER

ART DIRECTOR
Robert Miles Runyan
DESIGNER
Michael Mescall
ILLUSTRATOR
Michael Mescall
AGENCY/STUDIO
Robert Miles Runyan
& Associates
▲

ART DIRECTORS
Tom Antista
Petrula Vrontikis
DESIGNERS
Tom Antista
Petrula Vrontikis
ILLUSTRATOR
Tom Antista
CLIENT
Andresen Typographics
AGENCY/STUDIO
Antista Design

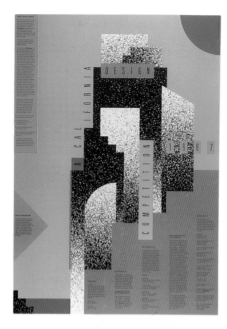

ART DIRECTOR
Jim Berté
DESIGNERS
Edie Garrett
Jim Berté
CLIENT
OBUNSHA CORP.
AGENCY/STUDIO
Robert Miles Runyan
& Associates
▲

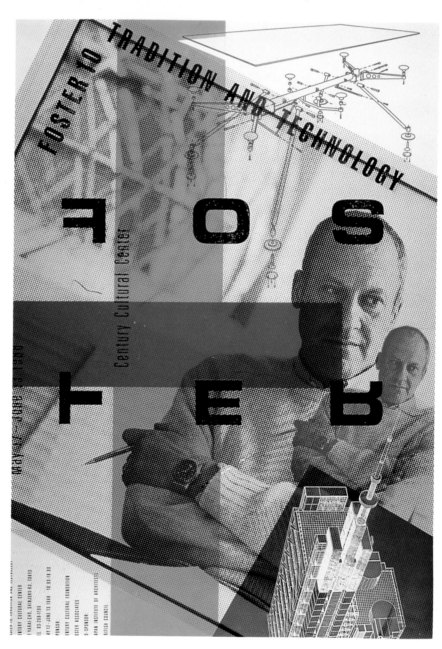

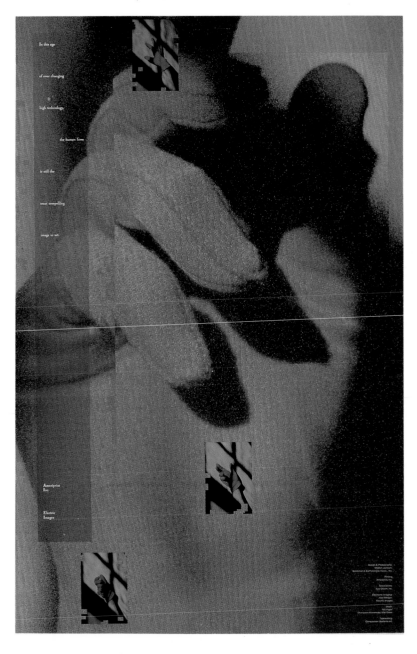

POSTER

ART DIRECTOR
Morton Jackson

DESIGNER
Morton Jackson

PHOTOGRAPHER
Morton Jackson

CLIENT
Ameriprint /
Electric Images

AGENCY / STUDIO
Sparkman &
Bartholomew Associates

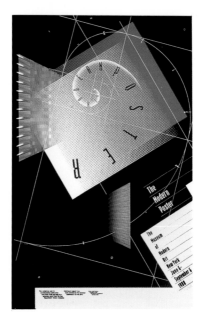

DESIGNER
April Greiman

CLIENT
MoMA
The Museum
of Modern Art

AGENCY / STUDIO
April Greiman, Inc.
▲

ART DIRECTOR
William Anton

DESIGNER
William Anton

PRINTER
anagrapics

TYPOGRAPHER
Print & Design

WRITERS
Eric Pick
Paul Rosenblatt

ILLUSTRATOR
William Anton

CLIENT
NYC/AIA

AGENCY / STUDIO
Chermayeff &
Geismar Associates

POSTER

ART DIRECTOR
Rochelle Gray

CREATIVE DIRECTOR
Catherine Seay

WRITER
Meredith Light

ILLUSTRATOR
Richard Waldrep

CLIENT
Washington Ad Club

AGENCY/STUDIO
Williams Whittle

PRODUCTION COMPANY
S&S Graphics
▲

ART DIRECTOR
Jennifer E. Morla

DESIGNERS
Jennifer E. Morla
Marianne Mitten

WRITER
Jennifer E. Morla

ILLUSTRATOR
Jennifer E. Morla

CLIENT
Mercury Typography

AGENCY/STUDIO
Morla Design
▲

ART DIRECTOR
Karl Bornstein

ILLUSTRATOR
Kristen Funkhouser

CLIENT
Mirage Edition

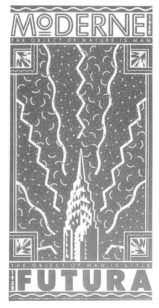

POSTER

ART DIRECTOR
Gerald Bustamante
DESIGNER
Gerald Bustamante
ILLUSTRATOR
Gerald Bustamante
CLIENT
Bicycling West, Inc.
AGENCY/STUDIO
Studio Bustamante

ART DIRECTOR
Gerald Bustamante
DESIGNER
Gerald Bustamante
ILLUSTRATOR
Gerald Bustamante
CLIENT
Bicycling West, Inc.
AGENCY/STUDIO
Studio Bustamante
▲

one hundred seventy seven

POSTER

ART DIRECTOR
Ken Eskenazi

DESIGNER
Ken Eskenazi

ILLUSTRATOR
Hauqua

CLIENT
David Kamansky
Pacific Asia Museum

AGENCY/STUDIO
Kaiser McEuen Inc.
▲

ART DIRECTOR
Rex Peteet

DESIGNER
John Evans

ILLUSTRATOR
John Evans

CLIENTS
Sibley/Peteet Design

ART DIRECTOR
Robert Appleton

DESIGNER
Robert Appleton

CLIENT
Real Art Ways

AGENCY/STUDIO
Appleton Design Inc.

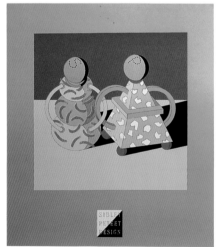

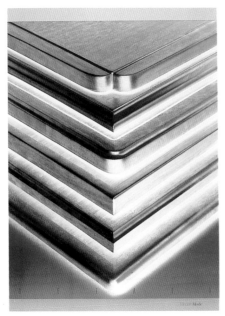

**Louise Fili
Douglass Scott
Jane Kosstrin
Bruno Monguzzi**

ART DIRECTOR
Dennis Thompson
DESIGNERS
Dennis Thompson
Veronica Denny
PHOTOGRAPHER
Steve Underwood
CLIENT
Modern Mode
AGENCY/STUDIO
The Thompson
Design Group

POSTER
ART DIRECTOR
Richard Poulin
DESIGNER
Mieko Oda
WRITER
Richard Poulin
CLIENT
Cooper Union School
of Art
AGENCY/STUDIO
de Harak & Poulin Assoc.
PRINTER
Rapoport Printing
Corporation

DESIGNER
April Greiman
CLIENT
Museo Fortuny
AGENCY/STUDIO
April Greiman, Inc.

POSTER

ART DIRECTOR
John C. Crane

DESIGNER
Dan Auvil

DIRECTOR
John C. Crane

WRITER
John C. Crane

PHOTOGRAPHER
Staff

ILLUSTRATOR
Les Leggett

CLIENT
Crane Dunker

AGENCY/STUDIO
Crane/Auvil

ART DIRECTOR
Lon Clark

DESIGNER
Linda Clark

WRITER
Stephen Clark

PHOTOGRAPHER
Lon Clark

ILLUSTRATOR
Heather Elmer

CLIENT
E.D. Bullard

AGENCY/STUDIO
Lon Clark Associates
▲

ART DIRECTOR
Guido Brouwers

DESIGNER
Guido Brouwers

WRITER
Joyce Brouwers

ILLUSTRATOR
Mark Smith

CLIENT
SmithBrouwers Inc.

AGENCY/STUDIO
THEY Design

The Fabric of Life

MENU, CALENDAR,
ANNOUNCEMENT
ART DIRECTOR
Kerry Walsh
DESIGNER
Kerry Walsh
WRITER
David Halpern
PHOTOGRAPHER
Oklahoma Chapter,
American Society of
Magazine Photographers
CLIENT
Tulsa Litho Company
AGENCY/STUDIO
Phillips Knight
Walsh, Inc.

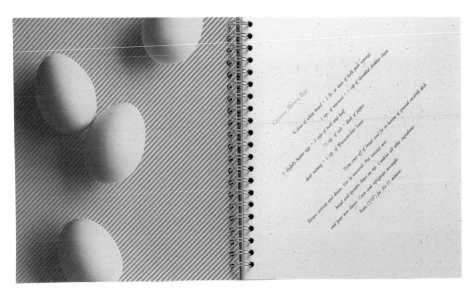

ART DIRECTORS
Pat Samata
Greg Samata
DESIGNERS
Pat Samata
Greg Samata
WRITER
Nancy Bishop
PHOTOGRAPHER
Mark Joseph
ILLUSTRATOR
Paul Thompson
CLIENT
Samata Associates

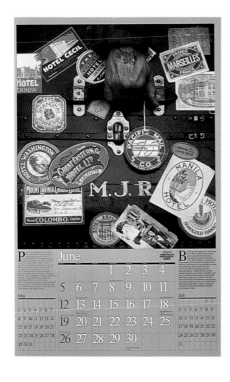

ART DIRECTOR
Kit Hinrichs
DESIGNER
Kit Hinrichs
WRITER
Peterson & Dodge
PHOTOGRAPHER
Terry Heffernan
ILLUSTRATOR
Sara Anderson
(Retouching)
CLIENT
American President
Companies
AGENCY/STUDIO
Pentagram Design

*MENU, CALENDAR,
ANNOUNCEMENT*

ART DIRECTOR
Tom Antista

DESIGNER
Petrula Vrontikis

PRODUCERS
Tom Antista
Thomas Fairclough

DIRECTOR
Tom Antista

CLIENT
Antista Design

AGENCY/STUDIO
Antista Design

ART DIRECTOR
Ken White

DESIGNER
Diane Foug

WRITER
Aileen Farnan Antonier

ILLUSTRATOR
Diane Foug

AGENCY/STUDIO
White & Associates

SELF PROMOTION

ART DIRECTOR
Neil Shakery

DESIGNERS
Neil Shakery
Natalie Kitamura

WRITER
David Gibbs

PHOTOGRAPHER
Henrik Kam

CLIENT
Pentagram Design

AGENCY/STUDIO
Pentagram Design
▲

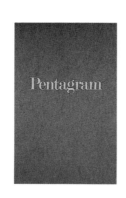

SELF PROMOTION

ART DIRECTOR
Jim Heimann

DESIGNER
Jim Heimann

ILLUSTRATOR
Alexander Vethers
(Cover)
Jim Heimann (Inside)

CLIENT
Margarethe Hubauer,
Artists Rep. —Hamburg

AGENCY/STUDIO
Jim Heimann

ART DIRECTOR
Scott Ray

DESIGNER
Scott Ray

WRITER
Mary Keck

ILLUSTRATOR
Scott Ray

CLIENT
Dallas Society of Visual
Communications

AGENCY/STUDIO
Peterson & Company
▲

SELF PROMOTION

ART DIRECTOR
Michael Hall

DESIGNER
Michael Hall

DIRECTOR
Michael Hall

WRITERS
Michael Hall
Debra Kelley

ILLUSTRATORS
Michael Hall
Martin Lawler

CLIENT
Hall Kelley, Inc.

AGENCY/STUDIO
Hall Kelley, Inc.

PRODUCTION COMPANY
Wallace-Carlsen

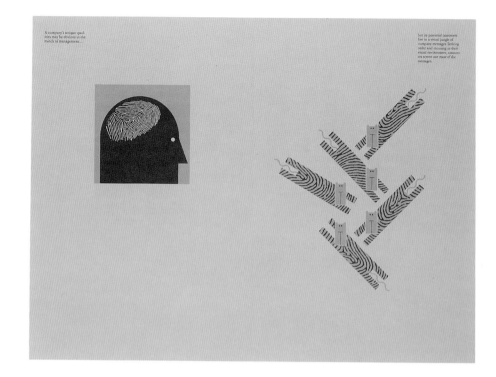

ART DIRECTOR
James Cross

DESIGNER
Yee-Ping Cho

WRITER
Various

PHOTOGRAPHER
Various

ILLUSTRATOR
Various

CLIENT
Simpson Paper Company

AGENCY/STUDIO
Cross Associates
▲

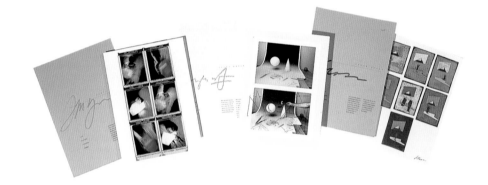

Good Tidings   Good Will   Good Wishes   Good Cheer   Good Design

Good Tidings

SELF PROMOTION

ART DIRECTOR
Van Hayes
WRITER
Van Hayes
ILLUSTRATOR
Van Hayes
CLIENT
Good Design
AGENCY/STUDIO
Good Design

Familiar objects.

Unique observations.

Inventive conclusions.

ART DIRECTOR
James Cross
DESIGNER
James Cross
PHOTOGRAPHER
James Cross
CLIENT
Cross Associates
AGENCY/STUDIO
Cross Associates

ART DIRECTOR
Scott Eggers
DESIGNER
Scott Eggers
WRITER
Mark Perkins
PHOTOGRAPHER
Gerry Kano
CLIENT
Kano Photography

*Any time you take a
picture for corporate use,
it puts the public image
of the corporation at risk.*

That's exposure.

CATALOG

ART DIRECTOR
James Sebastian

DESIGNERS
James Sebastian
Junko Mayumi

INTERIOR DESIGNER:
William Walter

PHOTOGRAPHER
Bruce Wolf

CLIENT
Martex/West Point
Pepperell

AGENCY/STUDIO
Designframe Inc.

PRODUCTION COMPANY
Designframe Inc.

▲

ART DIRECTORS
Bill Kobasz
Arlene Lappen

DESIGNERS
Bill Kobasz
Arlene Lappen

WRITER
Charlie Stainback

PHOTOGRAPHER
Various

CLIENT
International Center of
Photography/Midtown

AGENCY/STUDIO
Reliable Design
Studios, Inc.

ELLEN BROOKS
DETAIL FROM COLUMN (SIX HEADS)
1986-1987

DAVID BUCKLAND
THE NUMEROLOGIST (MATTHEW HAWKINS)
1984

ART DIRECTOR
Dennis Tani

DESIGNER
Dennis Tani

PRODUCER
Ovsey Gallery

WRITER
Robert Pincus

ARTIST
Ron Rizk

CLIENT
Grand Rapids
Art Museum

AGENCY/STUDIO
Dennis Tani Design Inc.

CATALOG

ART DIRECTOR
Paul Marciano

DESIGNER
Donna Eble

PRODUCER
Guess? Inc.

PHOTOGRAPHER
Neil Kirk

ILLUSTRATORS
Sharon Goldfarb
Christa Munro

AGENCY/STUDIO
Teamwork Design
▲

What is sexy?

ART DIRECTOR
Tamotsu Yagi

DESIGNER
Tamotsu Yagi

WRITER
Doug Tompkins

PHOTOGRAPHERS
Toscani (Image)
Roberto Carra (Still Life)

CLIENT
Esprit

AGENCY/STUDIO
Esprit Graphic Design

Is fashion fun and style serious?

ART DIRECTOR
Tamotsu Yagi

DESIGNER
Tamotsu Yagi

WRITER
Doug Tompkins

PHOTOGRAPHERS
Toscani (Image)
Roberto Carra (Still Life)

CLIENT
Esprit

AGENCY/STUDIO
Esprit Graphic Design
▲

BROCHURE, FOLDER

ART DIRECTORS
Tom Antista
Petrula Vrontikis

DESIGNER
Petrula Vrontikis

WRITER
Aileen Farnan Antonier

PHOTOGRAPHER
Henry Blackham

CLIENT
Surface Design
Technology

AGENCY/STUDIO
Antista Design

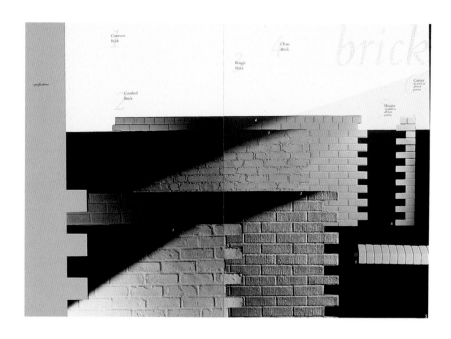

ART DIRECTORS
Rob Gemmell
Rob Price
Tim Brennan

DESIGNER
Jill Savini

PRODUCER
Kendra Plat

DIRECTORS
Rob Gemmell
Rob Price
Tim Brennan

WRITER
Rob Price

PHOTOGRAPHERS
Will Mosgrove
Roger Allen Lee

PRINTER
Anderson Lithograph

CLIENT
Apple Computer, Inc.

AGENCY/STUDIO
Apple Computer
Creative Services

PRODUCTION MANAGER
Kendra Plat

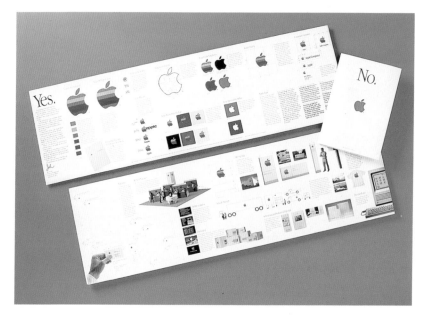

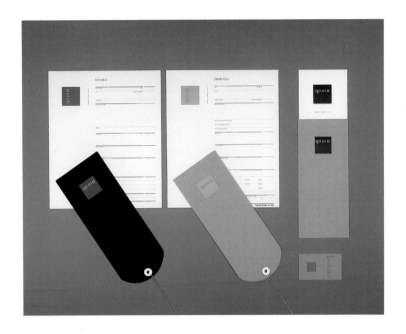

VISUAL IDENTITY

ART DIRECTOR
Benjamin Cziller
DESIGNER
Benjamin Cziller
CLIENT
Benjamin Cziller
AGENCY/STUDIO
Benjamin Cziller

ART DIRECTOR
Benjamin Cziller
DESIGNER
Benjamin Cziller
CLIENT
Mari Chikami
AGENCY/STUDIO
Cziller Design

ART DIRECTOR
Tom Antista
DESIGNER
Tom Antista
CLIENT
Dennis Mukai
AGENCY/STUDIO
Antista Design

VISUAL IDENTITY

ART DIRECTOR
Pat Zimmerman
DESIGNER
Pat Zimmerman
ILLUSTRATOR
Pat Zimmerman
CLIENT
Marten Mohr Associates
AGENCY/STUDIO
Pat Zimmerman
Advertising and Design

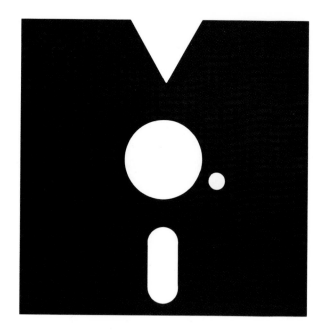

ART DIRECTOR
Margaret Youngblood
DESIGNER
Karen Smidth
CALLIGRAPHER
Gary Ferguson
CLIENT
Sitmar Cruises
AGENCY/STUDIO
Landor Associates

Sitmar Cruises

ENVIRONMENTAL
GRAPHICS

ART DIRECTOR
Michael Donovan

DESIGNERS
Michael Donovan
Susan Berman
Robert Henry

LIGHTING DESIGN
Richard Nelson

CLIENT
Brickel Associates, Inc.

AGENCY/STUDIO
Donovan and Green

PRODUCTION COMPANY
The Show Business
Group

EDITORIAL

EDITORIAL

BOOK DESIGN
COVER

ART DIRECTOR
Susan Mitchell

DESIGNERS
Keith Sheridan
Craig Warner

ILLUSTRATOR
Keith Sheridan

CLIENT
Random House, Inc.

AGENCY/STUDIO
Keith Sheridan
Assoc., Inc.

▲

ART DIRECTOR
Susan Mitchell

DESIGNERS
Keith Sheridan
Craig Warner

ILLUSTRATOR
Keith Sheridan

CLIENT
Random House, Inc.

AGENCY/STUDIO
Keith Sheridan
Assoc., Inc.

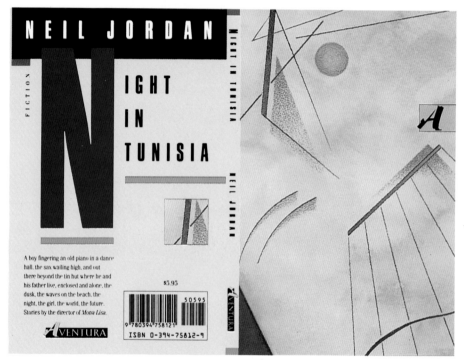

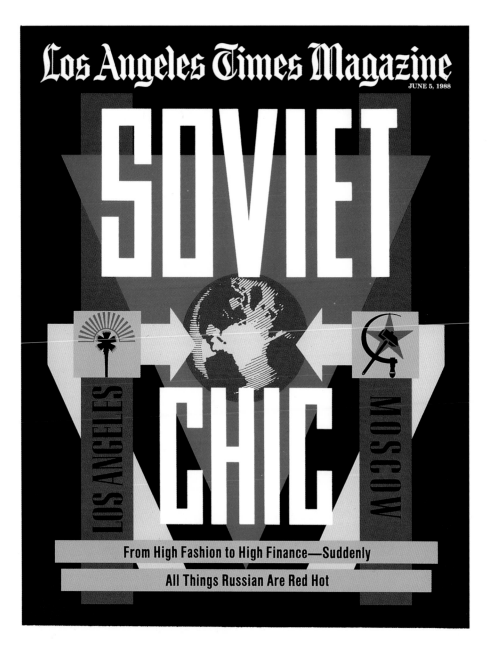

MAGAZINE DESIGN
COVER

ART DIRECTOR
Nancy Duckworth
DESIGNER
Jim Heimann
ILLUSTRATOR
Jim Heimann
CLIENT
L.A. Times
AGENCY/STUDIO
Jim Heimann

ART DIRECTOR
Nancy Duckworth
DESIGNER
Nancy Duckworth
PHOTOGRAPHER
Amedeo
CLIENT
Los Angeles Times
Magazine
AGENCY/STUDIO
DNA
PRODUCTION COMPANY
DNA

ART DIRECTOR
Matthew Drace
DESIGNER
Matthew Drace
PHOTOGRAPHER
David Peterson
AGENCY/STUDIO
San Francisco Focus

MAGAZINE DESIGN

ART DIRECTOR
Michael Brock

DESIGNER
Michael Brock

PHOTOGRAPHER
Cindy Lewis

CLIENT
Auto Gallery Publishing

AGENCY/STUDIO
Michael Brock Design

ART DIRECTOR
Michael Brock

DESIGNER
Michael Brock

PHOTOGRAPHER
Marvin Carlton

CLIENT
Auto Gallery Publishing

AGENCY/STUDIO
Michael Brock Design

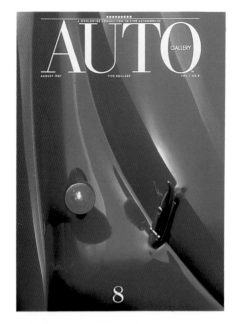

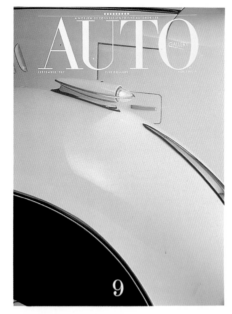

ART DIRECTOR
Michael Brock

DESIGNER
Michael Brock

PHOTOGRAPHER
Bruce Miller

CLIENT
Auto Gallery Publishing

AGENCY/STUDIO
Michael Brock Design

ART DIRECTOR
Michael Brock

DESIGNER
Michael Brock

PHOTOGRAPHER
John Paul Endress

CLIENT
Auto Gallery Publishing

AGENCY/STUDIO
Michael Brock Design

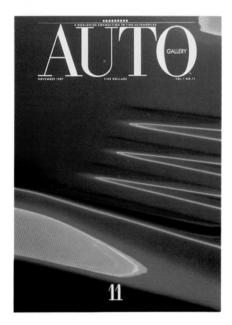

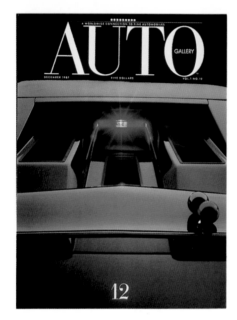

ART DIRECTORS
Henry Brimmer
Charly Franklin

DESIGNER
Henry Brimmer

PHOTOGRAPHER
Charly Franklin

CLIENT
Photo Metro

AGENCY/STUDIO
Henry Brimmer Design

ART DIRECTORS
Jack Anderson
John Hornall

DESIGNERS
Jack Anderson
John Hornall
Julie Tanagi
Jani Drewfs

WRITER
Orin Ziv

PHOTOGRAPHER
Steve Young

CLIENT
Egghead Software

AGENCY/STUDIO
Harnall Anderson
Design Works

PRINTER
Craftsman Press

MAGAZINE DESIGN

ART DIRECTOR
Nancy Montgomery
DESIGNER
Nancy Montgomery
PHOTOGRAPHER
Ann Revenge
AGENCY/STUDIO
Flowers & Magazine

ART DIRECTOR
Joe McNeill
DESIGNER
Steven D. Merin
ILLUSTRATOR
Dan Cosgrove
AGENCY/STUDIO
CMP Publications

MAGAZINE DESIGN

ART DIRECTOR
Matthew Drace
DESIGNER
Mark Ulriksen
PHOTOGRAPHER
George Steinmetz
LOGO DESIGN
Tim Carroll
Readers Guide
Lets Eat
Burritos

AGENCY/STUDIO
San Francisco Focus

In the
HEAT
of the
KITCHEN

Fifteen years ago, he arrived in Berkeley with $7 in his jeans, walked into Chez Panisse and started a food revolution. Now he's fighting for a restaurant of his own.

One evening last June, the drab, warehouselike interior of Pier 3 at Fort Mason was transformed into something more elegant for one of San Francisco's largest and most successful charity events – the Aid & Comfort benefit dinner. A blue-chip crowd of more than a thousand paid $250 a person to sample fifteen dishes prepared by the top chefs of the

BY BRIAN ST PIERRE & MARTY OLMSTEAD

THE POWER OF Tower: He couldn't get everything he wanted at Alice's restaurant, so Jeremiah Tower took his toque and opened Stars.

FINE DINING GUIDE 3

READERS, ENVELOPE *Please*

BY JACQUELINE KILLEEN AND SHARON SILVA

All year long we reviewers have had the floor in the great Bay Area restaurant debate. Now we've heard your side. Tallying the ballots tells us as much about you, our readers, as it does about your favorite restaurants. You're strong on eateries born in the past decade; only a handful of the winners are into their teens. And you seem to be steadfastly loyal to the same places, year after year. Yet there are some surprise winners in the poll – including a few restaurants that have been around barely a year. We learned that you speak your mind, too. Our omission of categories for American and Cambodian cuisines brought justifiably outraged grumbles from the fans of Cajun cooking, the Cambodia House restaurant and Campton Place. Our apologies; we hereby award write-in first places to both.

SAN FRANCISCO FOCUS *FINE DINING GUIDE 11*

LET'S *Eat*

BY WENDY JO JESTER

Ready for dinner? Or lunch? Tapas or high tea perhaps? Turn the page. Our critics have been eating nonstop for the past year just so you won't go hungry. And they've discovered over seven hundred restaurants to recommend in Northern California. Looking for Burmese food in the East Bay? Tortillas in Tahoe? A French bistro open late at night? We've got it. So what are you waiting for?

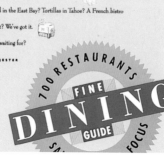

SAN FRANCISCO FOCUS

BURRITOS *And* BEAUJOLAIS?

BY NORM ROBY

Maybe not—but if you want wine with an ethnic meal, there are some mixed marriages that work.

San Francisco has long been recognized as the ethnic restaurant capital of the United States. It's also the unofficial, yet uncontested, center for people who know and appreciate fine wines. For anyone here who enjoys good food and wine, then, the question arises: Is wine really a good companion to a spicy, exotic meal? If so, which wines go best with what? The answer to the first question is yes, usually – if you have confidence in your own palate and an open mind. To arrive at a good marriage between wines and ethnic foods, you need to observe one rule: forget the rules. Start by rejecting that often misunderstood maxim of red wine with meat, [Continued on Page 20]

12 FINE DINING GUIDE SAN FRANCISCO FOCUS

MAGAZINE DESIGN

ART DIRECTOR
Doug Renfro
DESIGNER
Tim Frame
WRITER
Suzanne Harper
PHOTOGRAPHER
E.J. Camp
ILLUSTRATOR
Various
AGENCY/STUDIO
Whittle
Communications

EDITORIAL

MAGAZINE DESIGN
ART DIRECTOR
Matthew Drace
DESIGNER
Matthew Drace
PHOTOGRAPHER
David Peterson
AGENCY/STUDIO
San Francisco Focus

THE INTERVIEW
BY KEN KELLEY

LUIS VALDEZ

The director/playwright talks about new film, old theatre, Mayan mysteries—and those nasty New Yorkers

W

hen you're hot, you're hot. And when you're as sizzling hot as a grade-A jalapeño pepper on the grill, your name is Luis Valdez.

Proof: You've got a smash hit, summer-release feature film—*La Bamba*, the story of Ritchie Valens, the first crossover Latino rock 'n' roll star, who died at age seventeen in the same plane that killed Buddy Holly and the Big Bopper. Ritchie's early life echoes your own—a teenage farmworker picking the seasonal California harvest decides to pick a different *kind* of crop as

PHOTO-ILLUSTRATION BY ELISABET ZEILON

THE FOUR TOPS

JOANNA BERMAN

W

hile many of her colleagues at the San Francisco Ballet devoted this past summer's six-week layoff to guest appearances, vacationing or practicing at the barre, Joanna Berman spent much of the time knocking on wood.

Despite a persistent hip ailment, she went into this last San Francisco Ballet season—the most grueling experience of her tender professional life—as a promising local talent and emerged one of its brightest, most versatile young stars. Berman was virtually everywhere in the repertoire last winter. And artistic director Helgi Tomasson thought so much of her that he paired her with his new superstar Jean-Charles Gil for the opening night gala's *Tchaikovsky Pas de Deux*.

Knowing of Tomasson's background at Balanchine's New York City Ballet, Berman had a flash of panic. "I grew up thinking all New York City Ballet dancers were 5' 10" and 90 pounds, and here I was, quickly approaching 5' 5" and somewhere between 90 and 200 pounds, imagining Helgi wouldn't like my body type."

Her worries were groundless. Once she shed a bit of baby fat, Berman's conventionally female body type and her theatrical attack have endeared her to most resident and visiting choreographers.

You can't miss *Joanna Berman* these days, and you shouldn't.

ALLAN ULRICH

THE FOUR TOPS

RINDE ECKERT

H

e's tall and bald and he looks a good deal like an overgrown elf, especially when he jerks, writhes and flops his body about in quirky, contorted, polyrhythmic dances. But when Rinde Eckert opens his mouth to sing it's as if there's an angel inside.

Eckert is the renaissance man of San Francisco's experimental theatre, new music and modern dance scenes.

Early this spring, Eckert and performance artist Ruth Zaporah were being showered with accolades for their portrayals of a pair of inventively eccentric globe-wandering oldsters in their jointly created *Nomad Motel* at the Intersection. Shortly thereafter, mime Leonard Pitt opened at Life On The Water in the acclaimed *Not For Real*, directed and co-created by Eckert. The next thing anybody knew, Eckert was at Theatre Artaud, performing his libretto for *Was Are/Will Be* and *Shelf Life* with Paul Dresher and the Margaret Jenkins Dance Company; then he popped up at the Berkeley Repertory Theatre as an eerily winsome opium addict in Bertolt Brecht's *Good Person of Szechuan*.

Reviewing Eckert's work with the Paul Dresher Ensemble (he wrote and performed the libretto for Dresher's multilayered, spiraling score in the opera *Slow Fire*), *Newsweek* critic Alan Rich called him "one of that small body of authentic new music heroes." But that's just the tip of the Eckert iceberg. Writing, singing, composing, directing, acting—there's simply no telling where he'll turn up next.

ROBERT HURWITT

MAGAZINE DESIGN

ART DIRECTOR
Doug Renfro

DESIGNER
Bill McKenney

WRITER
Candyce Norvell

PHOTOGRAPHER
Bonnie Schiffman

ILLUSTRATOR
Various

AGENCY/STUDIO
Whittle
Communications

MAGAZINE DESIGN

ART DIRECTOR
Matthew Drace

DESIGNER
Matthew Drace

ILLUSTRATOR
Blair Drawson

AGENCY/STUDIO
San Francisco Focus

They were worlds apart, she thought.

Like Mother, Like Son

Fiction by
Joan Vincent
Cupples

[CONTINUED ON PAGE 63]

ART DIRECTOR
Deb Hardison

DESIGNER
Deb Hardison

DESIGN DIRECTOR
Bett McClean

WRITER
Pam Gerhardt

PHOTOGRAPHER
Lynton Gardiner

CLIENT
Whittle
Communications

AGENCY/STUDIO
Business Group

TYPESETTER
Composition Services

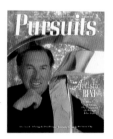

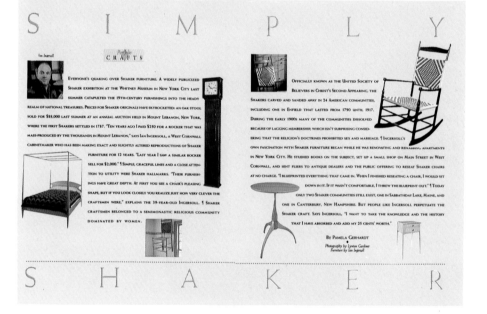

SIMPLY

Portfolio
CRAFTS

Everyone's quaking over Shaker furniture. A widely publicized Shaker exhibition at the Whitney Museum in New York City last summer catapulted the 19th-century furnishings into the heady realm of national treasures. Prices for Shaker originals have skyrocketed: an oak stool sold for $88,000 last summer at an annual auction held in Mount Lebanon, New York, where the first Shakers settled in 1787. "Ten years ago I paid $250 for a rocker that was mass-produced by the thousands in Mount Lebanon," says Ian Ingersoll, a West Cornwall cabinetmaker who has been making exact and slightly altered reproductions of Shaker furniture for 12 years. "Last year I saw a similar rocker sell for $2,000." ¶ Simple, graceful lines and a close attention to utility were Shaker hallmarks. "Their furnishings have great depth. At first you see a chair's pleasing shape, but if you look closely you realize just how very clever the craftsmen were," explains the 39-year-old Ingersoll. ¶ Shaker craftsmen belonged to a semimonastic religious community dominated by women.

Officially known as the United Society of Believers in Christ's Second Appearing, the Shakers carved and sanded away in 24 American communities, including one in Enfield that lasted from 1790 until 1917. During the early 1900s many of the communities dissolved because of lagging membership, which isn't surprising considering that the religion's doctrines prohibited sex and marriage. ¶ Ingersoll's own fascination with Shaker furniture began while he was renovating and rehabbing apartments in New York City. He studied books on the subject, set up a small shop on Main Street in West Cornwall, and sent fliers to antique dealers and the public offering to reseat Shaker chairs at no charge. "I blueprinted everything that came in. When I finished reseating a chair, I would sit down in it. If it wasn't comfortable, I threw the blueprint out." ¶ Today only two Shaker communities still exist, one in Sabbathday Lake, Maine, and one in Canterbury, New Hampshire. But people like Ingersoll perpetuate the Shaker craft. Says Ingersoll, "I want to take the knowledge and the history that I have absorbed and add my 25 cents' worth."

By Pamela Gerhardt
*Photography by Lynton Gardiner
Furniture by Ian Ingersoll*

SHAKER

ART DIRECTOR
Bett McClean

DESIGNER
Jonathan Tuttle

WRITER
Christine Palm

PHOTOGRAPHER
Bob Wagner/Onyx

CLIENT
Whittle
Communications

AGENCY/STUDIO
Business Group

TYPESETTER
Composition Services

The **CHAMPION** of **CHESS**

Modern sociology tells us that children are pawns—set back by poverty, conquered by ignorance, and taken by urban despair. But in chess a different set of rules governs the game. Pawns are allowed to move forward—never backward—albeit only one square at a time. Certainly they are the weakest pieces on the board. But placed strategically, their progress unchecked, they can capture even the strongest piece.

It is fitting, then, that in New York City, a retired executive named Fanueil Adams Jr. is using chess to help young people move forward with confidence and grace. Through a free program he started, called the Manhattan Chess Club School, urban children are learning how to play the game—where to place the pieces and how to make the smart moves.

Fanueil Adams believes that the strategies and skills learned in chess offer young people a way to move forward in life.

For Adams, to play chess is to surrender to its power. The game offers black-and-white choices; every action has a consequence, every move a countermove.

By Christine Palm
Photography by Bob Wagner/Onyx

MAGAZINE DESIGN

ART DIRECTOR
Doug Renfro
DESIGNER
Tim Frame
WRITER
Don Akchin
PHOTOGRAPHER
Bonnie Schiffman
ILLUSTRATOR
Various
AGENCY/STUDIO
Whittle
Communications

MAGAZINE DESIGN
ART DIRECTOR
Doug Renfro
DESIGNER
Bill McKenney
WRITER
Jackie Kaufman
PHOTOGRAPHER
Various
ILLUSTRATOR
Various
CLIENT
Whittle
Communications
AGENCY/STUDIO
Whittle
Communications

SAN FRANCISCO
The Center of Western Civilization

By Mark K. Powelson

PHOTOGRAPH BY GEOF KERN

INSIDE

Albert Besmanoff, known here and there as William Fortune, William Best, Al Best, and Albert Larry Berger, was a small-time loser, chronic faker, and liar who made the mistake of putting his fibs on blank checks. In the autumn of 1934, after spending about a third of his thirty-five years in various cages, Besmanoff-Fortune-Berger-Best finally made it to the big time: He was selected under his favorite name, Al Best, for charter membership in the criminal elite of North America. On the hearty recommendation of his warden, he was transferred from a minor federal lockup on the outskirts of Washington, DC, to the just-opened federal penitentiary at the center of San Francisco Bay.

ALCATRAZ

THE PRISON MEMORIES OF INMATE NUMBER 107: THE UNTOLD STORY OF AL CAPONE ON THE ROCK.

EDITED BY RICHARD REINHARDT

MAGAZINE DESIGN

ART DIRECTOR
Matthew Drace

DESIGNER
Mark Ulriksen

ILLUSTRATOR
Anthony Russo

CLIENT
San Francisco Focus

ART DIRECTOR
Matthew Drace

DESIGNER
Matthew Drace

PHOTOGRAPHER
Geof Kern

AGENCY/STUDIO
San Francisco Focus

ART DIRECTOR
Matthew Drace

DESIGNER
Mark Ulriksen

ILLUSTRATOR
Matt Mahurin

AGENCY/STUDIO
San Francisco Focus

EDITORIAL

MAGAZINE DESIGN

ART DIRECTOR
Doug Renfro

DESIGNER
Bill McKenney

WRITER
Jackie Kaufman

PHOTOGRAPHER
Various

ILLUSTRATOR
Various

CLIENT
Whittle
Communications

AGENCY/STUDIO
Whittle
Communications

MAGAZINE DESIGN

ART DIRECTOR
Tom Staebler

DESIGNER
Bruce Hansen

ILLUSTRATOR
Blair Drawson

CLIENT
Playboy

ART DIRECTOR
Tom Staebler

DESIGNER
Len Willis

ILLUSTRATOR
Robert Giusti

CLIENT
Playboy

ART DIRECTOR
Tom Staebler

DESIGNER
Eric Shropshire

ILLUSTRATOR
Michel Guire Vaka

CLIENT
Playboy

EDITORIAL

MAGAZINE DESIGN

ART DIRECTORS
Barry Shepard
Miles Abernethy

DESIGNER
Miles Abernethey

WRITER
Peterson & Dodge

PHOTOGRAPHER
Rodney Rascona

ILLUSTRATOR
Carol Hughes

CLIENT
Audi of America, Inc.

AGENCY/STUDIO
SHR Design
Communications

PHOTO|DESIGN
FOR THE CREATIVE TEAM

WHITE HOT!

WHO'S FASTEST IN THE FAST LANE? FROM LOS ANGELES TO
NEW YORK TO ICELAND, CELEBRITY PHOTOGRAPHER TIMOTHY
WHITE AND HIS CREW ARE HOT AND GETTING HOTTER.

By Jon Bowermaster

Nick Ashford and Valerie Simpson are twenty year veterans of the music business. They've penned hits for Diana Ross and Marvin Gaye, produced records with Gladys Knight and Chaka Khan, and recorded a dozen albums of their own. Still, this rainy day in April, they are having their picture taken and they are nervous. Just the day before, after a month of planning, they tried to back out of the shoot, claiming they "just weren't ready."

Dressed in black and posed cheek-to-cheek in a pale ochre and leafy green lounge near the rafters of Radio City Music Hall, they are skittish—like a pair of thoroughbred horses banging around their stalls pre-race. Pins have fallen from Simpson's antique dress exposing too much skin, Ashford calls for more powder. The room is hot, the talent is too, but the photographer is cool.

Crouched on his knees six feet in front of the songsters, Timothy White waits out their last

Left: The Tim White Show featuring (left to right) Vicky Godby, business manager; Timothy White; Russell Ward, first assistant; Trish Sands, studio manager.
Right: Bette Midler from a shoot for Home Box Office.

These days his friends call his life "The Tim White Show," and it features a cast
of hundreds from Phil Collins to Phil Donahue.

minute stallings, patiently. *He* should be the one who is nervous. He hopes to shoot them in five or six different setups and this is only the first. They want to leave by six. That gives him three hours. But he's used to the regimen. In the last three weeks he's made eighteen flights to shoot forty celebrities: from Iceland to New York to Germany to the Caribbean and back home to New York. But his patience is not a veneer—twelve hours to shoot James Woods and Sean Young, and sat on another until a Laker's basketball game was over in order to photograph Don Johnson. In fact, he is absolutely thrilled to be in this position and his renowned energy (his agent calls him "Mr. Adrenaline") is just kicking in.

The shoot begins.

"Perfect. Again.
"Perfect. Again.
"Look at Valerie. Nick. Nice. Same shot. Just like that.
"Nick, remember, give me half a second, don't move.
"Again.
"Perfect. Again. Only two more.
"Again.
"One more roll.
"That's nice. Smile. Big. Ohh, I like that.
"Only twelve more shots.
"Perfect."

After eight rolls White gets to his feet, smiling broadly. He runs a hand through his shoulder-length black mane, silver bracelets jangling. "That was great," he applauds. Ashford and Simpson respond in unison. "Wow, that was great." The nervousness has disappeared and the loveliest has begun. While his crew disassembles and moves to the next location, the photographer schmoozes with the stars, and soon they are chatting like long-lost friends, about business, music, sex, babies and real estate. Then they are off to change, and White is into the men's lounge, to map his next shot. On his way he crumples a Polaroid and without looking lofts it over his shoulder, smack

dab into a nearby ashtray. But he's moving too fast to notice his own good luck.

It has been that kind of year for Timothy White. It began with occasional "Random Notes" assignments from *Rolling Stone* and now Paul Newman and Sidney Poitier are leaving messages on his machine, praising his pictures of them. Bette Midler gave him three minutes, had so much fun she came back for more, and approved 51 of the 52 shots he sent her. *Esquire* and *Condé Nast's Traveler* had him shoot covers, *Us* calls four times a week and *Rolling Stone* has sent him from Austria (the U.S. ski team) to Jamaica (Ziggy Marley) to Iceland (The Suger Cubes).

"I've never had a photographer that has been able to get as many different situations out of a single portrait as he has," claims *Parade* art director Brent Peterson. "He even got Lee Iacocca to squeeze into a little clay car."

"He did five assignments in a row for me that were very, very good. Interesting, alive, vibrant pictures. That kind of consistency is very unusual," insists Victoria Kohn, a picture editor at *Us*.

"Timothy has developed more than any of our photographers in the last year," brags his agent Daniel Roebuck, whose L.A.-based Onyx agency represents the crème de la crème of the celebrity photographers crop, including Mark Hanauer, Bonnie Schiffman, Aaron Rapaport, E. J. Camp and William Coupon.

"The bottom line," says friend and former employer Chris Callis, "is that he's a fun guy with incredible energy and charm. People like him and respond to him and it shows in his pictures."

"The real bottom line," counters Kohn, "is that Timothy White is hot. Last year the hot celebrity photographer was George Lange, this year it's Karen Keuhn. Next year? Timothy."

"The fact that he is hot is not merely a question of style or accident though," says agent Roebuck with finality. "it's the result of consistently taking better pictures each time out."

From the top: Benny Cliff album cover, CBS Records; Allen Weisberg, designer; JoAnn Lennon album cover, Atlantic Records; Deb DeRosa, designer; Wailea Townley album cover; Palograms Records; Michael Bays, designer; Loki Jeremy Cliff from CBS album cover shoot; Painted backdrop by Vicky Godby.

MAGAZINE DESIGN

ART DIRECTORS
Barry Shepard
Miles Abernethy

DESIGNER
Miles Abernethy

WRITER
Peterson & Dodge

PHOTOGRAPHER
Robert Landau

CLIENT
Audi of America, Inc.

AGENCY/STUDIO
SHR Design
Communications

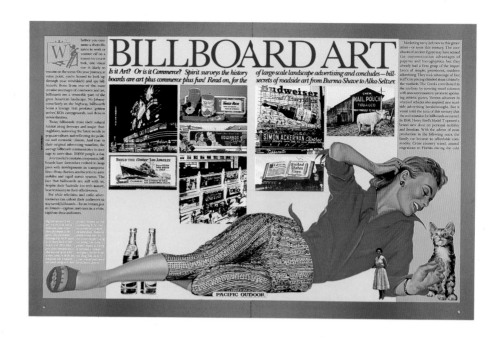

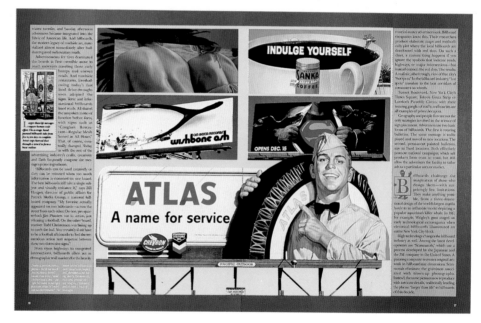

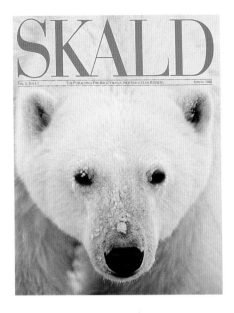

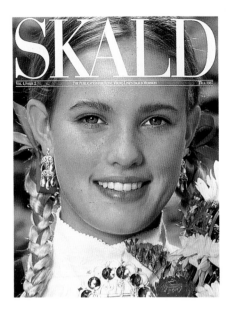

MAGAZINE DESIGN

ART DIRECTOR
Kit Hinrichs

DESIGNERS
Kit Hinrichs
Karen Berndt

WRITER
George Cruys (Editor)

PHOTOGRAPHERS
Harvey Lloyd
Barry Robinson

ILLUSTRATORS
Tim Lewis
Dugald Stermer
Mark Summers
David Linn

CLIENT
Royal Viking Line

AGENCY/STUDIO
Pentagram Design

ART DIRECTOR
Kit Hinrichs

DESIGNERS
Kit Hinrichs
Karen Berndt

WRITER
George Cruys (Editor)

PHOTOGRAPHERS
Michele Clement (Cover)
T. Heffernan
B. Robinson
H. Lloyd

ILLUSTRATORS
Dave Stevensen
Mark Summers
Michael Bull

CLIENT
Royal Viking Line

AGENCY/STUDIO
Pentagram Design

A DELECTABLE JOURNEY

It's not just armies that travel on their stomachs. Properly chronicled, the course of history marches right through potato fields, artichoke beds, vineyards, and big bowls of turtle soup.

ITALY, THE TWINING VINE

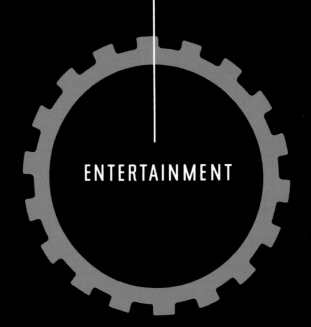

ENTERTAINMENT

MOTION PICTURE-PRINT

ART DIRECTOR
Ron Michaelson

DESIGNERS
Lucinda Cowell
Gunher Stotz

CLIENT
Island Pictures

AGENCY/STUDIO
Concept Arts

ART DIRECTOR
Ron Michaelson

DESIGNER
Lucinda Cowell

ILLUSTRATOR
Lucinda Cowell

CLIENT
Island Pictures

AGENCY/STUDIO
Concept Arts

C104-21

ART DIRECTOR
Brian D. Fox

DESIGNER
Clive Baillie

COMPUTER GRAPHICS
Electric Paint

PHOTOGRAPHER
F. Duhamel

CLIENT
De Laurentiis
Entertainment Group/
Michele Reese

AGENCY/STUDIO
B.D. Fox & Friends, Inc.

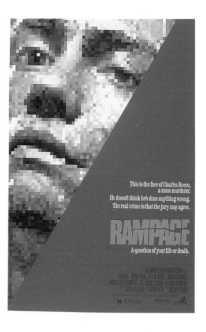

"WHO FRAMED ROGER RABBIT"

EXECUTIVE PRODUCER
Robert Jahn
PRODUCER
Craig Murray
*POST PRODUCTION
SUPERVISOR*
John Chambers

PRODUCER
Paula Silver

CREATIVE DIRECTOR
Christine Ecklund

WRITER
Kate Cox

CLIENT
Vestron Pictures

PRODUCTION COMPANY
R. Greenberg
and Associates

"DIRTY DANCING"

ANNCR: The dancing sets her free.

ANNCR: Vestron Pictures presents "Dirty Dancing." She thought it would be just another summer vacation.

BABY: Who's that?

NEIL: Oh them, they're the dance people.

ANNCR: But it turns out to be the time of her life.

BABY: I can't even do the Merengue!

ANNCR: He teaches her what she can do.

BABY: You're wild...

FATHER: I'm not sure who you are, but I don't want you to have anything to do with those people again.

JOHNNY: Baby, I don't see you running up to Daddy telling him I'm your guy.

BABY: Well, with my father, it's complicated. I will tell him.

JOHNNY: I don't believe you, Baby.

ANNCR: She shows him all he can be.

PENNY: You got to stop it now.

JOHNNY: I know what I'm doing.

BABY: I'm scared of everything, most of all I'm scared of walking out of this room and never feeling the rest of my whole life the way I feel when I'm with you.

ANNCR: What they learn from each other feels too good to be wrong.

ANNCR: "Dirty Dancing," starring Patrick Swayze, Jennifer Grey, and Cynthia Rhodes. Get ready for the time of your life.

"THE DEAD"

One by one we're all becoming shades.

How long you locked away in your heart the image of your lover's eyes when he told you that he did not wish to live!

I've never felt that way myself towards any woman, but I know that such a feeling must be love.

Better to pass boldly into that other world, in the full glory of some passion, than fade and wither dismally with age!

Snow is falling faintly through the universe and faintly falling, like the descent of their last end, upon all the living and the dead.

PRODUCER
Gary Balionis

CREATIVE DIRECTOR
Christine Ecklund

CLIENT
Vestron Pictures

PRODUCTION COMPANY
Quartermoon
Productions

ENTERTAINMENT
MOTION PICTURE
TRAILER

DESIGNERS
Tony Silver
Sam Alexander
PRODUCERS
Tony Silver
Barbara Glazer
DIRECTOR
Barbara Glazer
WRITER
Kate Cox
CLIENT
Charles O. Glenn
AGENCY/STUDIO
Orion Picture
PRODUCTION COMPANY
Tony Silver Films, Inc. NYC

"COLORS"

RAP MUSIC UP: Colors, colors, colors…

VOICE #1: They've got Uzis, they've got shotguns.

VOICE #2: We're outnumbered, we're outgunned.

VOICE #3: They got access to any kind of weapon they want within 24 hours.

VOICE #4: Fighting over red or blue.

VOICE #5: Bleeding over open wounds.

VOICE #6: Dying over colors.

KID: There's always going to be gangs, man. There's always going to be fighting.

PENN: See that badge? I wear it. That's my job.

KID: You want me to walk away from this, man? I love them, they love me back.

RAP MUSIC UP AGAIN

ANNCR: The debts men owe. The price they pay. The fragile bonds that hold men together. The conflicts that tear them apart. It's not about black and white. It's about a shade of difference. A tone of meaning…a clash of colors.

Sean Penn. Robert Duvall. In a Dennis Hopper film. "Colors."

V.O: Breaking and entering, robbery, and now possible murder. What do ya got lined up for tonight?

NARR: Women think he's a menace.

WOODS: Why would you do that? Why…would you do that?

NARR: Try to think of a three-letter word for explosive.

BAD GUY: You're a cop. You gotta take me in.

WOODS: Well, there's some good news and there's some bad news.

WOODS: Get up! The good news is, yeah, you're right. I'm a cop and I gotta take you in…The bad news is, I've been suspended, and I don't give a…

SFX: SHOTGUN BLAST

NARR: "Cop." James Woods in the most startling performance of his career. With Lesley Ann Warren and Charles Durning. When a man cares too much, how far is too far?

"COP"

OPERATOR: What city, please?

KILLER: Like, I'm in Hollywood, and I want to report a murder.

WOODS: I'm Detective Sergeant Lloyd Hopkins, with the police department. It's about Julie Nemeyer.

WARREN: Yeah, actually I was thinking about calling you guys. I just didn't know what to say.

WOODS: Why did you kill her?

NARR: There's a dangerous man on the loose.

WOODS: All I care about is stopping this maniac before he kills again. Do you understand?

WOODS: Come on, Duds. Ya blew away the broad's date. The least you could do is drive her home.

NARR: His boss thinks he's trouble.

V.O.: If you go to the media,

BOSS: ...I'll crucify you.

V.O.: You had a bad day, didn't you?

WOODS: How could you tell?

DAUGHTER: You always shake just a little.

NARR: His friends think he's crazy.

DURNING: One day he's suspended from the force...

ART DIRECTOR
Martin Rabinovitch

PRODUCERS
Robert Farina
"Smitty"
Chris Arnold

DIRECTOR
Chris Arnold

WRITER
Marshall Drazen

EDITOR
Seth Gavin

CLIENT
Martin Rabinovitch

AGENCY/STUDIO
Atlantic Releasing

PRODUCER
Barbara Glazer

CREATIVE DIRECTORS
Denise Farley
Sharon Streger

WRITER
Mark Semugger

CLIENT
Vestron Pictures

PRODUCTION COMPANY
Tony Silver Films

"PARENTS"

ANNCR: Coming soon, Randy Quaid, Mary Beth Hurt, Sandy Dennis and director Bob Balaban bring you a fresh look at family life.

MOTHER: Hi...

ANNCR: The Leamle family is moving up in the world.

MOTHER: Rise and shine...

ANNCR: But something is eating at young Michael Leamle.

FATHER: You're not scared of your room are you? Michael, the cellar is dark, everything is dark at night.

ANNCR: His parents think Michael's problem is in his head. But Michael knows it's on his plate.

MICHAEL: What are we eating?

MOTHER: Leftovers, honey.

MICHAEL: Leftovers from what?

MOTHER: From the refrigerator.

MICHAEL: We've had leftovers every day since we moved here. I'd like to know what they were before they were leftovers.

FATHER: Before that, they were leftovers to be.

TEACHER: Michael, there's nothing to be frightened of.

SFX: SCREAM.

ANNCR: Now there's a new name for terror: "Parents."

MOTHER: Bed time...

"A WORLD APART"

NARR: A family never knows when the world around it is about to explode.

MX: "Twist" music. "Yeah, twist again, like we did last summer."

FATHER: I have to go away for a while…It's my work.

RADIO: The South African Government today announced the first arrests under the…90-Day Detention Act.

MAY: Is that a hiding place?

HERSHEY: You must keep it a secret, do you understand?

MAY: Are you the one who's been in jail?

MAN: Yes.

RADIO: The Act confers power on the security forces to detain people without trial…for up to 90 days with interrogation.

HERSHEY: May I see your warrant?

MAN: I don't need a warrant, Mrs. Roth.

NARR: In 1963, Diane Roth, wife…mother… journalist…was the first white woman to be imprisoned under the now-infamous 90-Day Detention Act.

MAY: Mommy, please don't go. Mommy, don't go. Mommy!

WOMAN: Have you heard from your father?

MAY: No, Ma'am.

V.O.: We know every meeting you attended… We saw you come, we saw you go.

HERSHEY: If you know so much, why don't you charge me?

HERSHEY: Why don't you show me the…

V.O.:…pictures of the 69 you murdered at Shopville.

MAY: Go away and leave me alone.

WOMAN: Your father and mother are brave people. You must be proud of them.

WOMAN: Everybody's depending on you.

V.O.: You followed me, tapped my telephone, had me arrested…

HERSHEY:…and then you want me to believe that you're going to come to a free and unprejudiced decision on my future? I do not trust you.

MAN: Then you have nothing left to trust.

NARR: Barbara Hershey as Diane Roth. Jody May as her young daughter Molly.

SFX: PEOPLE YELLING

NARR: A mother's love. A family's courage. "A World Apart."

ART DIRECTOR
Martin Rabinovitch
PRODUCERS
Chris Arnold
"Smitty"
Robert Farina
DIRECTOR
Chris Arnold
WRITER
Marshall Drazen
EDITOR
Seth Gavin
CLIENT
Martin Rabinovitch
AGENCY/STUDIO
Atlantic Releasing

PRODUCER
Marc Gerber

DIRECTOR
Marc Gerber

WRITER
DMB&B/
Entertainment/LA

CLIENT
Island Pictures

AGENCY/STUDIO
DMB&B/
Entertainment/LA

PRODUCTION COMPANY
DMB&B/
Entertainment/LA

"SLAM DANCE"

AUDIO:
MUSIC: I love you...
V/O: Hot Kiss
MUSIC: For sentimental reasons.
V/O: Cold Sweat. Last Chance. "Slam Dance."
Rated R.

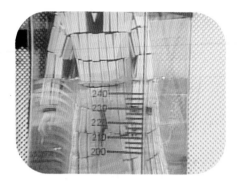

"LETTERMAN: SUIT WEEK"

ANNOUNCER VO: Tonight when you hear plop,
plop, fizz, fizz...
It means Dave is wearing the Alka Seltzer.
Late Night...Oh what a relief it is!

"LETTERMAN: SUIT WEEK"

ANNOUNCER VO: Tonight Dave has to suck
it up...
All 400 pounds of it...
When he tests the suit of sponges!
Late Night...It's totally absorbent!

"LETTERMAN: SUIT WEEK"

ANNOUNCER VO: Tonight you'll find David
Letterman extremely attractive...
Once he puts on the suit of magnets!
Tune in, but keep your canned goods away from
the set!

ART DIRECTOR
Nancy Paladino
DESIGNER
Nancy Paladino
PRODUCER
Miranda Knaub
WRITER
Miranda Knaub
CLIENT
Late Night with
David Letterman
PRODUCTION COMPANY
Electric Picture Works

TELEVISION-VIDEO

ART DIRECTOR
Carl Willat

DESIGNER
Mike Nichols

PRODUCER
Chris Whitney

DIRECTOR
Carl Willat

WRITERS
Mike Nichols
Carl Willat
Don Smith

PHOTOGRAPHERS
Bob Dalva
Melissa Mullin

ILLUSTRATOR
George Evelyn

CLIENT
The Disney Channel

AGENCY/STUDIO
Direct

PRODUCTION COMPANY
Colossal Pictures

"MR. MOUSE GOES
TO WASHINGTON"

AUDIO: Music track only.

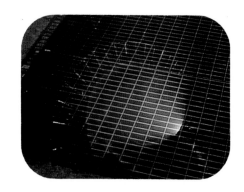

"BEAUTY & THE BEAST"

VINCENT: This is where the wealthy and the powerful rule.

It is her world.

A world apart from mine.

Her name is...Katherine.

From the moment I saw her, she captured my heart with her beauty...her warmth...and her courage.

I knew then, as I know now, she would change my life...forever.

KATHERINE: He comes from a secret place far below the city streets, hiding his face from strangers, safe from hate and harm.

He brought me there to save my life...

And now, wherever I go, he's with me in spirit.

For we have a bond stronger than friendship or love. And although we cannot be together, we will never, ever be apart.

ART DIRECTOR
Jeff Bacon

EDITOR
Phillip Terrance

PRODUCERS
Robert Farina
Chris Arnold

DIRECTOR
Robert Farina

WRITER
Marc Paykuss

CLIENTS
Tony Thomas
Paul Witt

AGENCY/STUDIO
Witt, Thomas

...AINMENT

)S

...RECTORS
...eiden
Margo Chase
DESIGNER
Margo Chase
CLIENT
Warner Bros.
Records, Inc.

ART DIRECTOR
Tommy Steele
DESIGNER
Andy Engel
ILLUSTRATOR
Andy Engel
CLIENT
Capitol Records

RECORDS
ILLUSTRATOR
Fraser McDermott
CLIENT
Dep Intnl. /
A&M Records

ART DIRECTOR
Bob Defrin
DESIGNER
Bob Defrin
ILLUSTRATOR
Michael Paraskeuas
CLIENT
Atlantic Records

ART DIRECTOR
Carol Bobolts
DESIGNER
Carol Bobolts
PHOTOGRAPHER
Matt Mahurin
CLIENT
Tracy Chapman /
Elektra Records

RECORDS
ART DIRECTOR
Deborah Norcross
DESIGNER
Deborah Norcross
ILLUSTRATOR
Deborah Norcross
CLIENT
Warner Bros. Records
AGENCY/STUDIO
Warner Bros. Records
In-House
▲

PAT METHENY GROUP
Still Life (Talking)

Collaboration
GEORGE BENSON/EARL KLUGH

MICHAEL FRANKS
The Camera Never Lies

jazz it up

ART DIRECTORS
Jeff Ayeroff
Margo Chase
DESIGNER
Margo Chase
ILLUSTRATOR
Margo Chase
CLIENT
Virgin Records
America, Inc.

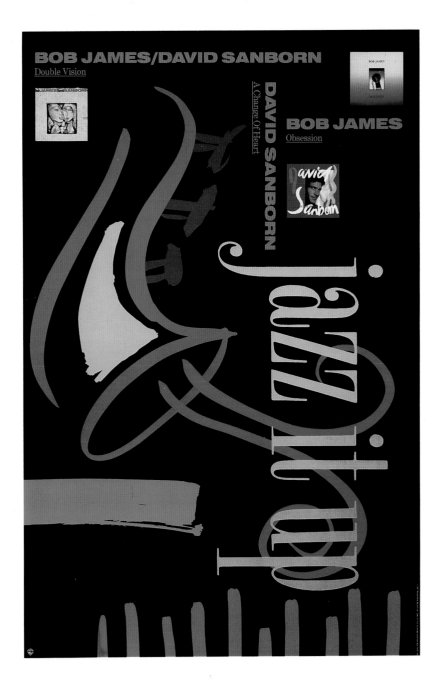

RECORDS

ART DIRECTOR
Deborah Norcross
DESIGNER
Deborah Norcross
ILLUSTRATOR
Deborah Norcross
CLIENT
Warner Bros. Records
AGENCY/STUDIO
Warner Bros. Records
In-House
▲

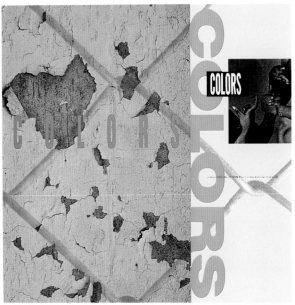

ART DIRECTORS
Jeri Heiden
Deborah Norcross
DESIGNER
Deborah Norcross
PHOTOGRAPHERS
David Skernick
Merrick Morton
CLIENT
Warner Bros. Records
AGENCY/STUDIO
Warner Bros. Records
In-House

HOME VIDEO
CREATIVE DIRECTOR
Russell Kelban
DESIGNER
Georgia Young
WRITER
Pamela Mason-Davey
CLIENT
Nelson Entertainment
AGENCY/STUDIO
Nelson Entertainment

HOME VIDEO
ART DIRECTOR
Lisa Robins
DESIGNER
Lisa Robins
ILLUSTRATOR
Mark Conahan /
Camerawork
CLIENT
Media Home
Entertainment
AGENCY/STUDIO
Media Home
Entertainment

INDEX

HOPPER PAPERS

FINE
COVER & TEXT
PAPERS

™CARDIGAN

®TAPESTRY

®CHAMBRAY

®DYNASTY

®LEGENDRY

®SKYTONE

®SUNRAY

®FELTWEAVE

WHERE TO FIND PERFECT HEADS
AND BODIES.

HEADS 1

ANDRESEN TYPOGRAPHICS HEADS 1

Start with Andresen's
new type books, a reference
standard of more than
6,000 typefaces.
Three volumes of heads.
Two volumes of bodies.
One better looking
than the other.

Separations by Techtron Los Angeles/Photography by Dan Arsenault

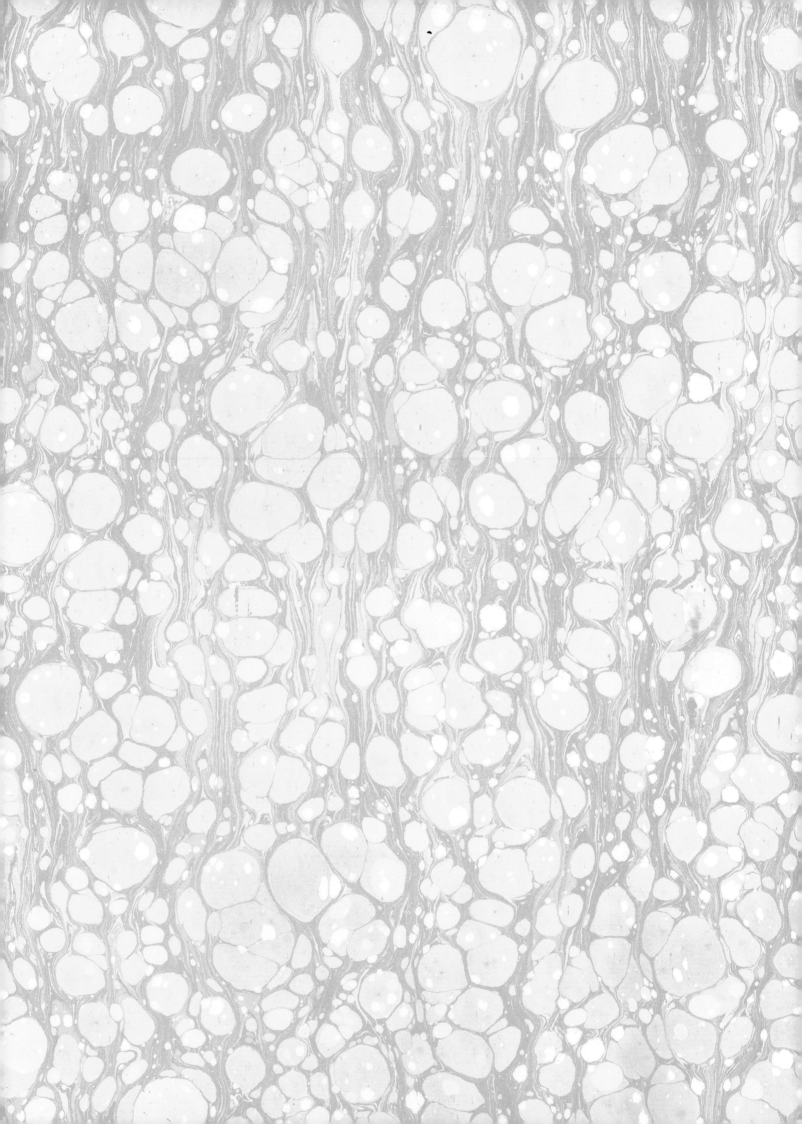